# THE BIRTH OF
# DEMOCRACY

## AN EXHIBITION CELEBRATING THE
## 2500TH ANNIVERSARY OF DEMOCRACY

## AT THE NATIONAL ARCHIVES, WASHINGTON, D.C.
## JUNE 15, 1993 - JANUARY 2, 1994

THE AMERICAN SCHOOL OF CLASSICAL STUDIES AT ATHENS
THE NATIONAL ARCHIVES, WASHINGTON, D.C.
THE MINISTRY OF CULTURE OF GREECE

CATALOGUE EDITED BY JOSIAH OBER AND CHARLES W. HEDRICK

"The Birth of Democracy"
The National Archives, Washington, D.C.
June 15, 1993 - January 2, 1994

Organized by the American School of Classical Studies at Athens'
"Democracy 2500 Project," in cooperation with
the National Archives and Records Administration

"Democracy 2500 Project"
Josiah Ober and Charles W. Hedrick, Co-Directors
Catherine Vanderpool, Associate Director

"The Birth of Democracy" Exhibition
Diana Buitron-Oliver and John McK. Camp II, Curators
Circulated by Art Services International
Designed by Michael Graves, Architect

"The Birth of Democracy" Catalogue
Josiah Ober and Charles W. Hedrick, Editors
Catherine Vanderpool, Coordinator
Diana Buitron-Oliver and John McK. Camp II, Authors
with contributions by
Alan L. Boegehold, Peter G. Calligas, William D. E. Coulson, Dina Peppa-Delmouzou,
Charles W. Hedrick, Carol Lawton, Josiah Ober, Jennifer Roberts,
Katerina Romiopoulou, Alan Shapiro, Andrew Szegedy-Maszak, Olga Tzachou-Alexandri
Drawing on title page depicting "Law against Tyranny" by Michael Graves, 1993.
Michael Graves, Architect, Designer
Nancy Wolfe, Production Coordinator

Photos of material from the Agora Excavations were taken by Craig and Marie Mauzy.
Photos of material from other museum collections were provided by the individual museums.

The exhibition has been funded in part by a grant from the National Endowment for the Humanities,
and is also supported by an indemnity from the Federal Council on the Arts and the Humanities.
This exhibition was first shown in Athens with the support of the A. G. Leventis Foundation.

The catalogue has been underwritten by a generous grant from
The Morris and Gwendolyn Cafritz Foundaton.

ISBN 87661-950-2.

*For Doreen Canaday Spitzer*
*Mentor and Friend*

# ACKNOWLEDGEMENTS

This catalogue and the exhibition of which it is a record have their roots in a series of discussions initiated by Doreen C. Spitzer, President Emeritus of the Trustees of the American School of Classical Studies at Athens. Initiated in 1988, these discussions led to a planned series of public programs formally inaugurated as the "Democracy 2500 Project" by the School's Trustees and Managing Committee the next year. Since that time the Project's Directors have incurred a great many debts to individuals and to institutions; it is a pleasure to be able to acknowledge some of them here.

Hunter Lewis, President of the Trustees, and Alan Boegehold, Chairman of the School's Managing Committee, have provided the Project with executive and academic oversight. It fell to Catherine Vanderpool, Associate Director of the "Democracy 2500 Project" and now Director of U.S. Operations for the School, to assume a central role in the administration of the Project from the beginning; without her energy, dedication, and diplomatic finesse the Project would never have gotten off the ground. John McK. Camp II, the School's Mellon Professor of Archaeology, and Diana Buitron-Oliver dedicated uncounted hours to their role as Co-Curators. William D.E. Coulson added the many burdens involved with the Project to his already extensive portfolio of responsibilities as Director of the School in Athens.

The staff of the School in Athens, New York and Princeton has been essential to our efforts: Jan Jordan, Secretary for the Agora Excavations; the conservators Alice Paterakis and Olympia Theophanopoulou; Maria Pilali, Administrative Assistant in Athens; in New York, Ludmila Schwarzenberg, Margaret-Anne Butterfield, and Christine Klein; and in Princeton, Nancy Moore and Susan Potavin. Craig Mauzy, Manager of the Agora Excavations, and Marie Mauzy were responsible for the splendid color photography of the objects from the Athenian Agora.

We would also like to thank our Greek colleagues, who have been of utmost importance at every step of the way: Katerina Romiopoulou, Director of the Department of Prehistoric and Classical Antiquities of the Ministry of Culture of Greece; Peter G. Calligas, Director of the "A" Ephoreia of Prehistoric and Classical Antiquities; Olga Tzachou-Alexandri, Director of the National Archaeological Museum in Athens; and Dina Peppa-Delmouzou, Director of the Epigraphical Museum in Athens. Also in the Ministry of Culture we would like to express our thanks to S. Boutoupoulou and A. Lembesi; in the National Museum, N. Prokopiou; and in the "A" Ephoreia, M. Kyrkou, all of whom have been extremely helpful.

We are most grateful to the many lenders to the exhibition outside of Greece as well: Dr. Wolfgang Oberleitner and Dr. Alfred Bernhard-Walcher at the Antikensammlung of the Kunsthistorisches Museum in Vienna; Dr. Roger Moorey and Dr. Michael Vickers at the Ashmolean Museum in Oxford; Dr. Wolf-Dieter Heilmeyer at the Staatliche Museen zu Berlin, Antikensammlung.

In the United States we thank John Walsh, Marion True, and Karen Manchester at The J. Paul Getty Museum; Alan Shestack, Cornelius Vermeule, and Florence Wolsky at the Museum of Fine Arts, Boston; Peter Kuniholm of the Department of the History of Art at Cornell University; Morteza Sajadian, Jane Biers and Jeff Wilcox at the Museum of Art and Archaeology of the University of Missouri, Columbia; Philippe de Montebello, and Carlos Picon, at the Metropolitan Museum of Art, New York; Robert Dyson and David Romano at the University Museum, University of Pennsylvania; Alan Rosenbaum and Michael Padgett at The Art Museum, Princeton University. In addition, we extend our thanks to other individuals who helped in various aspects of the exhibition: Henry Immerwahr, Barry Strauss, Homer Thompson, Susan Matheson, Richard Keresey, and Alice Whelihan.

The exhibition would not have been possible without the active help, support, and patience of our colleagues at the National Archives and Records Administration. Linda Brown, Assistant Archivist for Public Programs; Edith James, Director, Exhibits and Educational Programs Division; Emily W. Soapes, Chief, Exhibits Branch; Christina Rudy-Smith, Exhibits Curator; Allan Kaneshiro, Exhibit Designer; James Zeender, Registrar; and Paula Nassen Poulos, Adult Education Specialist, have all worked unflaggingly over the past two years on every aspect of the exhibition.

Our gratitude also to Art Services International, Lynn K. Berg, Director, and Joseph W. Saunders, Chief Executive Officer, for their expertise in solving the many logistical challenges of this international effort; to Donna Eliot, Registrar; and to the staff at Michael Graves, Architect for their creative energies, especially Patrick Burke and Lorissa Kimm.

We would also like to thank Steven Koob for his assistance with conservation issues; Jerome Eisenberg of Minerva Magazine for his advice; Gonda Van Steen for her translation of Mrs. Alexandri's essay.

Major funding for the exhibition was provided by the National Endowment for the Humanities, and for the catalogue by a generous grant from The Morris and Gwendolyn Cafritz Foundation. The exhibition was also supported by an indemnity from the Federal Council on the Arts and the Humanities. We would also like to acknowledge the generosity of the A.G. Leventis Foundation for their assistance in supporting the exhibition during its Athens appearance.

Josiah Ober
Charles W. Hedrick
Co-Directors, "Democracy 2500 Project"

# LENDERS TO THE EXHIBITION

Agora Museum, Athens
National Archaeological Museum, Athens
Epigraphical Museum, Athens

The J. Paul Getty Museum
The Museum of Fine Arts, Boston
Department of the History of Art, Cornell University
Museum of Art and Archaeology, University of Missouri, Columbia
The Metropolitan Museum of Art
The University Museum, University of Pennsylvania
The Art Museum, Princeton University

Antikensammlung, Kunsthistorisches Museum, Vienna
Ashmolean Museum, Oxford
Staatliche Museen zu Berlin, Antikensammlung

# TABLE OF CONTENTS

# INTRODUCTORY REMARKS
## I. THE ATHENIAN REVOLUTION

JOSIAH OBER
PRINCETON UNIVERSITY
CO-DIRECTOR, "DEMOCRACY 2500 PROJECT"

As we enter the last decade of the twentieth century, Democracy is the political watchword. The word "democracy" has not always been regarded in such a positive light, but it has finally won out over its competitors: monarchy, the rule of the one; aristocracy, the rule of the so-called "best"; and oligarchy, the rule of the wealthy. Today democracy has come to be virtually synonymous with fair, free, government; the last quarter of the twentieth century could quite easily be designated "The Age of Democracy" by future political historians. Thus it is a very happy coincidence that the decade of the 1990s (specifically 1993) will mark democracy's 2500th anniversary.

Some time in the year that spanned July of 508 to July of 507 B.C., a Spartan army marched to the independent city-state of Athens at the behest of a few disgruntled Athenian aristocrats. After seizing control of the city the Spartans then attempted to replace Athens' governing Council with a pro-Spartan puppet government. This was too much for the ordinary citizens of Athens, who suddenly and violently rose up in arms against the army of occupation. The citizens defeated and expelled the Spartans and the Athenian quislings who had called them in. The popular uprising of 508 B.C., an assertion of the collective will of the mass of the citizenry against the schemes of the selfish few, can properly be called the Athenian Revolution. Its consequences were as profound as the better known revolutions of our era— 1776, 1789, 1917, or 1989. In the immediate aftermath of the successful revolution, Kleisthenes of Athens responded to the revolutionary energy of the day by devising a radically new type of government. The Greeks dubbed it *Demokratia*, "rule by the people."

About eighty years after the reforms of Kleisthenes, at a public funeral held for Athenian soldiers killed in war, a politician-general named Perikles was chosen to deliver the customary speech over the warriors' ashes. He spoke about the bravery of the fallen, and he spoke of the democracy they had died to defend:

> Our constitution does not copy the laws of neighboring states; we are a pattern to others, not imitators ourselves. Its administration is by many instead of the few; that is why it is called a democracy. . . . Here each individual is interested not only in his own affairs, but also in the affairs of the state; even those who are mostly occupied with their own businesses are extremely well-informed on general politics—for unlike any other nation we do not say that a man

1

who has no interest in politics is unambitious; we say that he is useless.

Granted that this is an idealizing portrait of a highly complex society, Perikles' depiction sums up an important part of the Athenian democratic ideal: the sense of a shockingly new and influential political order that explicitly rejected the rule of a narrow elite in favor of the rule of the many, and which in turn asked each citizen to participate actively in public life or be regarded as useless. This system, born in popular revolution and sustained by the ideal of action for the common good, worked remarkably well. At the time of the overthrow of the democratic government by the vastly superior military forces of Macedon in 322 B.C., Athens had been a democracy for almost two hundred years. So far only the United States has managed to beat Athens' record by preserving an independent democracy for a longer time.

There is much that the modern democrat is likely to find repugnant about ancient Athens. Athenian women were systematically denied political citizenship; slavery was common and seldom questioned; defeated enemies were often treated brutally. But we would be indulging in absurdly anachronistic complacency if we were to refuse to learn from the Athenian experience of democracy on the grounds that their value system is at odds with that of the modern Western world. Democracy as it was practiced in ancient Athens can and should seem strange to us today, but there is an important connection between the ideals of ancient Athens and modern America. The Constitutional Framers of the United States were deeply influenced by the history of Athens and ancient political theory has had a lasting impact on modern political practices. When the Framers set out to create a new form of government in the late eighteenth century, they naturally looked to classical history for models. Since they had already rejected monarchy and aristocracy as possible forms of government, the two great ancient examples they confronted were the democracy of fifth and fourth century B.C. Athens and the republicanism of third and second century B.C. Rome.

In the end, the Framers rejected Athens in favor of Rome—in part because they knew Athens almost entirely through the study of ancient texts. Many of the texts written in classical Athens (e.g. the *History* of Thucydides, the *Republic* of Plato, the *Politics* of Aristotle) were overtly critical of democracy. Ironically, the democratic Athenian insistence on freedom of speech encouraged the production of critical writing which, while profound and thoughtful, served in the long run to obscure the positive achievements of the Athenian democratic government. That positive achievement can now be better appreciated thanks to the dedicated labor of modern archaeologists. Archaeology has helped to recapture some of the excitement, the strangeness, the uniqueness of the Athenian experiment with government by the ordinary citizens. The artifacts illustrated here can help us to forge a connection both with the citizens of Athens, and with those who were denied the status of citizenship. This catalogue and the series of interpretive essays which bracket it suggest some of the many ways that modern classical scholars are using texts and artifacts to rethink and better understand the meaning of ancient democracy.

But why is understanding democracy important? Despite the nearly universal affection for the term democracy, it is unlikely that most citizens of modern democratic nations would be able to agree on a single definition for the word. Democracy's tremendous success has come at a certain cost: the word "democracy" is now tossed around so loosely that for many citizens it may no longer signify much of anything. Rather than standing for a set of clearly articulated political values, the word "democracy" may be coming to stand for something so diffuse that few citizens will feel very strongly about it one way or the other.

The history of classical Athens may offer a cure for this semantic slide into vagueness. For the ancient Athenians, Demokratia meant that ordinary citizens (*demos*) hold the political power (*kratos*) in the state. In the sixth through the fourth centuries B.C. government "by the People" remained a startling notion—and there were always those who thought that the government should be by "the best," "the wealthy," or "the one." In order to sustain and defend their remarkable political regime the Athenians devised a flexible and sophisticated system of political institutions, including a popular citizen Assembly (*ekklesia*), a Council (*boule*) chosen by lottery, and People's Courts (*dikasteria*) staffed by hundreds of jurors. To ensure that important decisions were accessible to the whole of the citizenry, legislation was "published" through the erection of inscribed marble slabs in the public square. In order to ensure that the People had access to their laws, a state Archive was established in the Agora—the city's political center. But most important, those institutions were undergirded by a vibrant political culture: Athens worked as a democracy because the citizens engaged daily in the ongoing public conversation and action that constituted the practice of democracy.

Despite the Framers' doubts, Athenian Demokratia seems in some ways quite similar to modern American conceptions of government. Yet in other ways the Athenian approach to democratic government was surprisingly different from any modern political regime. Assessing the similar-ities and differences between ancient and modern democratic practices and ideals can help today's citizens sharpen their own definition of what democracy now is—and what they believe it should become. Close to two centuries after the Constitution was written, American lawmakers chartered the National Endowment for the Humanities with the words, "Democracy demands wisdom and vision in its citizens." The central goal of "The Birth of Democracy" and of this catalogue is to encourage citizens to think seriously about the meaning of democracy.

None of the diverse modern views of democracy in this collection is meant by the editors to be finally authoritative; indeed the various essays were written from very different points of view and they offer very different perspectives on ancient Athens. While diverse in how they read the significance of the ancient evidence, the multiple authors of this volume are united in their conviction that thinking about the ancient experience of democracy is a genuinely important matter today. The goal of the co-editors of this catalogue was not to impose a single, homogenized vision of classical Athens. Rather, we hope that the body of ancient texts and artifacts that is presented here, along with a variety of interpretations of that material, will help readers to refine their own understanding of the historical status and the future of democracy as a way of government and as a way of life.

# II. ATHENS AND AMERICA

WILLIAM D. E. COULSON
DIRECTOR
THE AMERICAN SCHOOL OF CLASSICAL STUDIES AT ATHENS

The years 1992-1993 mark the 2500th anniversary of one of the most important events in Western history: the democratic reforms of the Greek statesman Kleisthenes. In 508/7 B.C. the citizens of Athens, under the leadership of Kleisthenes, began instituting governmental reforms which set the basis for the democratic ideals influencing our lives even today. It was these democratic ideals that the founding fathers of the United States considered, along with those of Republican Rome, while writing the constitution some 200 years ago. It is particularly appropriate, therefore, that the exhibition, "The Birth of Democracy," should take place in the Rotunda of the National Archives in Washington, D.C., where the Declaration of Independence and the Constitution of the United States of America are displayed.

Thomas Jefferson was one of the earliest of the American philhellenes. Between 1784 and 1789 he was Minister to France, and in his last year in Paris he met the Greek writer and politician Adamantios Korais. The two became friends and corresponded regularly; in a letter dated July 10, 1823, Korais appealed to Jefferson for help in setting out the principles to guide Greece in establishing its own new government after independence. Jefferson replied on October 31, 1823, in a long letter setting out the principles of democratic government, mentioning such things as freedom of religion, freedom of the press, and in-

dividual rights. The writers of the American constitution were inspired by the Greek democratic ideal, and, in return, the Americans were among the first people to help the new Greek government in establishing its own democratic principles. Jefferson himself writes, "I cannot help looking forward to the re-establishing of the Greeks as a people and the language of Homer becoming again a living language." Our founding fathers, in fact, admired the ancient Greeks so much that they debated whether or not to adopt Greek as the official language of the new nation. In the ensuing debate, it took Benjamin Franklin to break the tie in favor of English.

It is also highly appropriate that this exhibition has been organized by the American School of Classical Studies at Athens. The American School was founded in 1881 in Athens, Greece, as a place "where young scholars might carry on the study of Greek thought and life to best advantage, and where those who were proposing to become teachers of Greek might gain such acquaintance with the land and such knowledge of its ancient monuments as should give a quality to their teaching unattainable without this experience," and where excavations and exploration of ancient sites and monuments might be conducted. These are still the aims of the School, but they have broadened over the century since Charles Eliot

Norton of Harvard University first conceived the idea of establishing a school in Greece to allow students to gain first hand experience of Greece in all periods of its history, from earliest times to the present. This public exhibition expands those aims, since it has been designed to address a broad, nonspecialist audience by bringing to light the classical past and by using this heritage to illuminate the present.

The majority of the objects in this exhibition come from the American School's excavations in the Agora of ancient Athens. The Agora was the civic and economic center of the old city, just as Washington is the center of political life in the United States today. The excavations, authorized in 1929 by a special act of the Greek Parliament, began in 1931 and continue to this day. They have uncovered evidence on how the reforms of Kleisthenes were actually carried out and on how democratic processes worked in the ancient city of Athens.

This 2500th anniversary of the birth of democracy in Greece marks a milestone in Western history. The American School of Classical Studies at Athens, in conjunction with the Greek Ministry of Culture and the National Archives and Records Administration, is proud to present this exhibition which it hopes will illustrate not only the close connections the United States has with Greece but also how important Greek thought has been in the formation of our own thinking and way of life. In order to emphasize these connections, this exhibition opened first in Athens at the American School's Gennadius Library before moving to Washington. Both the American School of Classical Studies and the Greek Ministry of Culture hope that you will enjoy this exhibition and use it as a stimulus to reflect upon the origins of our political heritage.

# III. DEMOCRACY AND FREEDOM

KATERINA ROMIOPOULOU
DIRECTOR OF PREHISTORIC AND CLASSICAL ANTIQUITIES
MINISTRY OF CULTURE, GREECE

Democracy is the constitutional formation that has its basis in human freedom. It is certainly no coincidence that the word, which originated in ancient Athens and passed virtually unchanged into every European language, becoming an integral part of them, signifies the cradle in which the pure spring of freedom is nurtured. For freedom, as understood by Greeks of today, and by all Europeans, is the indivisible freedom of the human being; the freedom to be found in human dignity, in the wisdom of the ancient Greek philosophers, in the beauty of ancient Greek sculpture, in the bitterness of fate in ancient Greek tragedy.

The image, as revealed to us by the works of the great Greek writers (philosophers, historians, poets), is that of political man. A spirit alien to the state was as inconceivable to the Greek of the fifth century B.C. as a state alien to the spirit. The greatest works of Hellenism are monuments of a political consciousness touched by a unique grandeur; a consciousness whose struggle advances in uninterrupted progression through all the stages of evolution, from the age of the heroes of the Homeric poems to Plato's *Republic* with its philosopher kings.

The fundamental truth of ancient Greek culture is that for the Greeks, humanism—to be a human being—is and always was bound up with our political nature. It is indicative of the close relationship between creative cultural activity and the community that the most distinguished of the ancient Greeks regarded themselves as pledged to the service of the social group, and acted as independent enlighteners of the people and shapers of its ideals. It is for this reason that the democratic constitution expresses better than any other formation the ideals of a community of free individuals, who desired their administrative organization to reflect their strong wish that the communal body should be a single, unified entity. Under the rule of *isonomia*—equality before the law—the social body (society) took the form of a circular, centralized world in which every citizen, as the equal of all the others, had to run the course to the end, holding and relinquishing in turn, in chronological order, all the balanced positions that constitute the world of politics.

For the Greek, and more specifically for the ancient Athenian, the individual could not be distinguished from the citizen. *Phronesis*—prudence—is the prerogative of free men exercising their political rights under the constraint of *logos*—reason. By providing the citizens with a framework within which they could comprehend their relationships with each other, political thought at the same time directed the steps of the spirit toward other spheres, such as philosophy and art.

6

# WRITING AND THE ATHENIAN DEMOCRACY

CHARLES W. HEDRICK
UNIVERSITY OF CALIFORNIA, SANTA CRUZ
CO-DIRECTOR, "DEMOCRACY 2500 PROJECT"

There is no practice more characteristic of the Athenian democracy than writing. From its inception in 508/7 B.C., the Athenian democracy emphasized "published" records of its political decisions and activities, framed in the formal, uniform phrases that would characterize state documents throughout the history of the democracy. Over time, the rate of "publication" of inscriptions by the state increased. Laws, decrees, catalogues of magistrates, lists of war dead, financial records of various sorts—the Athenians of the fifth and fourth centuries B.C. documented their political habits almost obsessively, compiling archives in perishable media as well as on durable marble. Documents kept on wood or papyrus have long since perished, but many of the inscriptions have survived. In fact, the number of fifth- and fourth-century Athenian inscriptions that have come down to modern times is unparalleled by any other ancient Greek state.

The temptation to explain the practice of writing with reference to the political system of the Athenians is irresistible. In the modern United States, of course, we understand writing and literacy to be prerequisites of democracy. If decisions are ultimately made by the people, the people must be informed in order to choose wisely. Documents should be accessible, and the people should be able to read them. By making texts available, by educating individuals, the United States produces citizens. It is thus virtually second nature for us to imagine that reading and writing are political skills necessary for any mass participation in government. Such is the prestige of literacy today that it is difficult to conceive how a democracy, or indeed any complex society, could function without a high rate of literacy.

The context of writing in ancient Greece was quite different from our own, and so, consequently, were feelings about it. Modern Americans are reared to be a nation of readers, and we tend to understand texts primarily as things to be read. It is unlikely, however, that the majority of Athenian citizens could read the inscriptions that their democracy erected. The orality of Athenian society raises difficult questions: If few could read, why did the state bother setting up inscriptions? What is the political force of a generally illegible public document? How would an illiterate citizen understand an inscription? The Athenian attitude toward writing was ambiguous: on the one hand, it was regarded as intrinsic to democratic practice; on the other hand, it was mistrusted as a powerful weapon with great potential for abuse. What was the role of inscriptions and the attitude toward them in a predominately oral society? How can we relate this gap between letters and the unlettered to the positive and negative political connotations of writing?

Many scholars have maintained that some rudimentary literacy was demanded of all Athenian citizens who participated in government. Procedures such as ostracism and the inscription of state documents, they argue, presuppose at least "name-signing" literacy from all. Some estimate a degree of literacy among Athenian citizens that is comparable or even surpasses that of contemporary industrial states, such as the United States. Yet based on comparative anthropological, sociological, and historical studies, it seems extremely unlikely that a majority of Athenian citizens could read. By modern standards, Athens was a traditional, agrarian society, and such societies are not known for producing large reading publics.

In addition, it is well known that the Athenian state did nothing to promote mass literacy: There was no state-subsidized education. In these circumstances, it is difficult to imagine how any significant number of Athenian citizens could have learned to read with any facility, if at all.

There are, to the contrary, many indications that Athenian politics and society of the fifth and fourth centuries were predominately oral. Virtually without exception, political practices—communication, deliberation, administration—were predicated on speech rather than on writing. Most of the vaunted Athenian literature, the famous dramas, poetry, philosophical essays, and histories, was written to be heard. Reading itself was an oral exercise, a social exchange, practiced aloud by individuals among groups of auditors, not a silent, private activity practiced in seclusion, as it usually is today.

Although many Athenians could not read, it was possible for inscriptions to communicate in other ways. The physical appearance of state documents was very homogeneous, governed by rigidly standardized guidelines. The very consistency of public texts made them immediately recognizable as a class, visually comprehensible as public pronouncements in a manner that was independent of the public's ability to read.

The democracy had developed a distinctive "chancellery style" for inscriptions by the mid-fifth century; it differed from the lettering styles used by other, contemporary Greek states and was also readily distinguishable from local Athenian writing styles used for private documents, such as ostraka, vases, and the like. This "chancellery style" governed every aspect of the appearance of the public inscription. The proportions of the stone stelai, or slabs, on which inscriptions were carved, were fixed; the Attic dialect of Greek, with its own distinctive orthography and letter forms, was standardized for use in these texts; even the physical layout of the letters on the stone was standardized.

As often in the ancient world (and for that matter, in the medieval and modern worlds), the development of a distinctive script goes hand in hand with the emergence and self-definition of a government. A particular script will often be limited to a particular political sphere of domination or influence. So, for instance, the regime of Charlemagne promoted the Carolingian minuscule; the Third Reich assumed the Gothic appearance of the Fraktur. As a script is promoted by a government, so it serves as the official badge of the government that promotes it. In a very general way, then, the distinctive Attic chancellery style is a recognizable sign of the democratic government of Athens.

One of the most distinctive and easily recognized features of official Attic inscriptions is the stoichedon style. The word *stoichedon* is an adverb meaning "in the fashion of rows." The text is inscribed in the pattern of a grid: the individual letters do not vary in size; there are no word, sentence, or paragraph divisions. Viewed as a whole, the text has (for connoisseurs, at least) an aesthetically pleasing, abstract appearance. But the stoichedon is not conducive to quick, easy reading. There is no attempt to organize the text into easily comprehensible visual units. The reader must ferret out words, phrases, sentences, and paragraphs, which have been dissolved into the regular, undifferentiated matrices of the stoichedon grid. It can be said, with some justice, that this is a style better seen than read.

In fact, the stoichedon style implies a certain kind of reading public. The organization of texts into semantic units by means of systematic word divisions, capitalization, punctuation, and the like began in the West in the twelfth and thirteenth centuries after Christ. This new, visual organization of the text accompanied, perhaps even made possible, the advent of the printing press, mass literacy, and modern internalized "silent reading." Texts without such visual aids, on the other hand, are characteristic of earlier medieval society, where literacy was quite restricted and reading took place orally, among groups of auditors. The stoichedon style, then, suggests a kind of audience and a mode of communication that differs fundamentally from modern readers and reading.

Beyond its standardized format, the physical character of a public inscription, its size and location, its simple presence conveyed certain meanings. Reading the frail, printed text of this essay, or the printed translation of the "Law against Tyranny," it is too easy to overlook the sheer weight and dimensions of an inscription, its architectural character. The physical presence of the inscribed stone in the inhabited urban space of the ancient world is one of the most important and least recognized differences between an inscription and our texts. In the modern world, we have forgotten what habits inscriptions foster. Even some seventy years ago inscribed monuments, such as lists of those killed in World War I, were commonly erected in the squares of many American and European towns. Most of our texts today, however, be they newspaper articles or scholarly essays, exist nowhere except in the limbo of endlessly identical, mass-produced print media. The topographical specificity of the monumental text has been lost. Ancient inscriptions, in their various shapes and sizes, with their different silhouettes and applied decorations, are as much *things* as they are *texts*, and their size, decoration, and topographical disposition echo and confirm meanings beside and beyond the letters they bear.

The emphasis that the Athenian democracy placed on inscribing its documents on stone tablets and erecting them in public places is remarkable and undeniable. The documents, however, were not displayed simply to be read, or even to be read at all, but to be accessible: As many inscriptions say, they are erected "so that anyone who wishes can inspect them." As M. I. Finley pointed out, in the absence of a "reading public" the inscrutable letters carved in marble stood as unequivocal reminders of public action, as silent but eloquent assertions that democratic power is not founded on secrets or deceit but is available to all. For the many citizens who were illiterate, it was not necessary to read the inscriptions; their monumental, physical presence was enough.

For the first one hundred years of the democracy, public documents were published only by inscribing them in stone and setting them up in the public space of the city. Then, at the end of the fifth century B.C., an archive was established in the Agora, in the Metroön, where records were kept on papyrus and other perishable materials, such as wooden planks. There probably was more or less complete public access to these archives; nevertheless, their establishment marks a vaguely sinister watershed in the history of political reading and writing in Athens. No longer were all public texts kept in monumental format, preserved as a matter of course as a part of the urban environment, where any casual passerby could see them, walk around them, or lean on them. Henceforth, some texts were kept out of sight.

When words are set down in writing, they seem to become fixed, unalterable, "carved in stone," so to speak. The ancient Athenians often thought of writing as providing a kind of egalitarian standard. Divorced from the dynamic, mercurial interplay of oral exchange, written proclamations are static and cannot be changed at will by the influential, powerful, or wealthy. Euripides provides a classic statement of this attitude. In one of his plays, he has Theseus, a mythical founder of Athenian democracy, say: "When laws have been written, both the weak man and the wealthy have an equal legal case, and the weaker if he is slandered may sue the more fortunate, and the weaker man, should he be in the right, defeats the strong man" (*Suppliants*, lines 433-37). The independence of written words from the give and take of oral society is not entirely benign, however. Protectors can easily become tyrants. Written laws can serve to equalize weak and strong, mass and elite, or they can be abused by the few to oppress the many.

The spoken word seems ideally democratic, immediate and transparent to all. Insofar as all are members of the same community, none are excluded from oral communication. Furthermore, speech apparently emanates immediately from conscious will and is an infinitely adaptable tool of representation. If confusion arises in conversation or debate, positions can be altered, attitudes adjusted, to suit the circumstances and the audience. If opponents misconstrue a statement, whether willfully or by error, their interpretation can be immediately corrected and controlled by the author.

Writing, unlike speech, is obviously not comprehensible to all members of the community. In addition, when once words are fixed on stone or papyrus, they cannot modify themselves according to the situation. They become dull, stupid—unable to respond. Removed from their author, they can give only one answer, always the same. So the written text is susceptible to abuse by the unscrupulous and the ignorant. Plato critiques writing for precisely these reasons, concluding:

> When words are once written down, they are tumbled about everywhere among those who may or may not understand them, and they do not know to whom they should speak, and to whom not; and if they are maltreated or abused, they always lack the help of their father; they cannot defend or help themselves. (*Phaedrus* 275d)

The written word is an alien thing, external to human consciousness and will. Even the laws of a democracy, once set in letters, are dislodged from the oral decision-making processes and the circumstances that generated them. No longer dependent for their power on popular will, they float free, an authority without an author, and can be appropriated by any who desire.

Writing, then, can be a democratic or a tyrannical force. It was perceived as both by the ancient Athenians. The only safeguard against the abuse of the laws lay in bridging the gap between oral and written expression. Plato makes just such an argument when he claims that writing is a destroyer when used as a substitute for memory; that it only has positive value when it interacts with human consciousness, when it serves as a supplement to memory, a reminder, a prompt (*Phaedrus* 276d-278b). Demosthenes, in the more political context of a speech written for a public trial, makes a similar point:

> And what is the strength of the laws? If one of you is wronged and cries out, will they run up and be at his side to help him? No. Letters are only written things, and they would not be able to do this. So what is their power? If you support them and make them ever powerful to help one who needs them. So the laws are strong through you, and you through the laws. (Demosthenes 21.224)

Thus the democratic power of writing lies not in its distant, authoritarian intelligibility, but in the active, social interaction of citizens, literate and illiterate, with the vague, inscrutable hieroglyphs that remind them and reassure them of what everyone already knows.

SUGGESTED READING:

M. I. Finley, "Censorship in Antiquity," *Times Literary Supplement*, 29 July 1977 (translated into Italian with expanded notes: Belfagor 32 [1977] 605-22)

W. V. Harris, *Ancient Literacy*, Harvard 1989

F. D. Harvey, "Literacy in the Athenian Democracy," *Revue des études grecques* 79 (1966) 585-635

R. Thomas, *Oral Tradition and Written Record in Classical Athens*, Cambridge 1989

A. G. Woodhead, *The Study of Greek Inscriptions* 2nd ed., Cambridge, 1981

# REPRESENTATIONS OF ATHENIAN DEMOCRACY IN ATTIC DOCUMENT RELIEFS

CAROL LAWTON
LAWRENCE UNIVERSITY

Historians of ancient art frequently note that Greek art, in its portrayal of contemporary or historical events, preferred indirect allusion to explicit depiction. The Greeks' use of allegory to generalize the specific and concrete and to transpose history into myth was a means of universalizing their human experience. The examples most familiar to students of Greek art are the frequent depictions after the Persian wars of such subjects as the Battles of the Greeks and Amazons and of the Lapiths and Centaurs, mythical conflicts in which Greeks or their allies repulsed non-Greek or beastly forces, to refer to the wars and to the cultural superiority of the Greeks over the barbarian Persians. But another regular and consistent use of allegory in the portrayal of contemporary events in Greek art is often overlooked. This is the depiction, in Athenian reliefs carved above official inscribed documents such as decrees, financial accounts, and laws, of gods, heroes, and personifications, embodiments of the states and parties with which the documents are concerned. The reliefs are of particular interest for students of Athenian democracy because in the fourth century B.C. they represented the Athenian state itself in the guise of the personified Athenian people and their democratic institutions.

The earliest document reliefs appeared in the 420s B.C. on marble stelai recording decrees concerning the foreign relations of the Athenian empire, but they are also found on public documents concerning domestic affairs, such as the business of financial boards and religious cults. They disappeared in the early third century, probably casualties of the same sumptuary legislation of Demetrios of Phaleron that apparently put an end to the Athenian production of grave and votive reliefs. In Athens the stelai were set up most frequently on the Acropolis but also occasionally in other sanctuaries and in the Agora.

With the exception of mortal worshippers and recipients of honors, almost all the figures in document reliefs are in some sense personifications, embodying cities, civic institutions such as the Athenian *ekklesia* and *boule*, and abstract concepts such as democracy. Their actions, usually consisting of handclasps and crowning with wreaths, refer to the relationships between the parties in the documents. The inscribed documents, recording the contemporary actions of the Athenian government, and their reliefs, depicting the events in symbolic terms, worked together to convey a message at the same time concrete and universal.

A look at one of the earliest fully preserved stelai with a relief illustrates how its relief describes, generalizes, and elevates the relationship of the parties involved and the historical situation that underlay it. (Fig. 1) The stele, erected in 403/2 B.C., records three Athenian decrees concerning their allies from the island of Samos at the end of the Peloponnesian War. The main provisions of the decrees, written in terse legislative prose, praise the Samians for their loyalty after the Athenian defeat at Aigospotamoi and grant the loyal Samians Athenian citizenship. The relief depicts Athens' patron goddess Athena, fully armed with helmet and spear, her shield resting against a tree behind her. She clasps the right hand of her Samian counterpart, the goddess Hera, queenly with her *stephane* and scepter. In the context of the inscription, the goddesses have stepped out of their mythological roles to become personifications of the Athenian and Samian participants in the agreement. The clasping of right hands, a motif called *dexiosis*, occurs frequently in document reliefs and signifies not merely formal agreement in the matter immediately under consideration but also the general concord and unity of purpose of the two allies. The overall picture conveyed by the stele is one of equality between the two parties and divinely inspired and protected cooperation in their shared endeavor. Contemporary Athenians and Samians would have understood this to have been their heroic last stand in the Peloponnesian War.

The Samian relief is typical of document reliefs of the fifth and early fourth centuries in its embodiment of Athens in Athena, but in the fourth century Athens and her interests are sometimes represented by the more specific personifications of Demos (the Athenian People and its Assembly), of Boule (the Council of the Assembly), and of Demokratia (Democracy).

Demos is securely identified by inscribed labels on two reliefs that probably originally belonged to honorary decrees (Figs. 2, 3); a similar but

Figure 1: *Athena and Hera representing Athens and Samos on an Athenian stele of 403/2 honoring the Samians. Athens, Acropolis Museum 1333. Photograph courtesy Acropolis Museum.*

unlabeled figure in other reliefs must represent the same personification (see page 152, Fig. 3). He is consistently depicted as an older, bearded, long-haired figure resembling typical representations of the gods Zeus and Asklepios. He is sometimes the same scale as Athena and always larger than the mortals he honors. While on the one hand he looks like a typical elder citizen of the city, the true embodiment of the people he represents, on the other hand his superhuman scale and his interaction with gods and heroes elevate him and the political entity he represents to a higher sphere.

The personification of Demos in these reliefs is more complex than it first appears. In the most literal sense, Demos stands for the technical use of the term *demos* in the decrees, which customarily began "resolved by the boule and demos of the Athenians." The demos in this case refers to the people of the ekklesia, the legislative body that ratified all Athenian decrees. In at least two reliefs (see page 152, Fig. 3, and page 154, Fig. 5), the inclusion of the personified Boule makes the reference to the two legislative institutions even more explicit.

But Demos sometimes also represents the broader sense of the word, the sense of demos as the entire Athenian people and its state, as it appears in the language of contemporary political speech and writing. This is the meaning of the Demos who appeared with Theseus and Demokratia in a famous, now lost, painting by Euphranor in the Stoa of Zeus Eleutherios in Athens, which depicted Theseus as the founder of Athenian democracy (described in Pausanias 1.3.3). The pairing of Demos and Demokratia in the painting indicates that Euphranor's Demos was intended as the whole Athenian people represented by the democratic constitution rather than the restricted sense of demos as ekklesia. And it is surely this Demos who is crowned by the personified Demokratia in the relief of the antityranny law of 337/6 (see page 152, Fig. 2). The figures in the relief refer directly to the content of the inscription, a law that seeks to protect "the demos of the Athenians" and "the democracy of Athens," that is, the people of Athens and their constitution. There can be no question of Demos as ekklesia in this relief, because the document is not a decree

Figure 2: *Demos, right, honoring a man named [----]-dron, from a stele of the second half of the 4th c. Athens, Epigraphical Museum 2791. Photograph courtesy Epigraphical Museum.*

passed by the demos of the ekklesia but a law ratified by the *nomothetai*, a board appointed by the ekklesia to judge proposals for new laws.

The personification of Demos in Athenian document reliefs, then, can have two meanings, and it is probable that in most reliefs (the antityranny stele being perhaps the single exception), Demos is to be understood in *both* the broad and restricted senses. He represents the citizens who enacted the decree, alliance, or other business recorded in the inscription, and at the same time he accompanies Athena as the embodiment of Athens and its people.

Boule is a simple personification, one perhaps invented for document reliefs, since there is no evidence of her in major sculpture or painting. She is also less popular, identifiable with certainty in only two reliefs in which she apparently accompanied Demos. In a relief from the second half of the fourth century, whose document has been lost (see page 154, Fig. 5), the female figure with Athena is identified by an inscribed label as Boule. Demos was probably originally present in the missing right half of the relief, since the boule that the female figure represents could not act independently in the business with which the documents were usually concerned. With her himation draped over her head like a veil, she resembles the bridal type of the goddess Hera, perhaps chosen to make her an appropriate counterpart to the Zeus-like Demos. A nearly identical figure appears with Athena and a figure conforming to the Demos type in the relief of a decree of 323/2 B.C. honoring a man named Asklepiodoros (see page 152, Fig. 3). The scale of Demos and Boule, intermediate between that of the mortal honored and Athena, is appropriate for their status as personifications.

Personification of abstract political concepts is rare in document reliefs, and Demokratia appears in only one, the relief of the antityranny law. But inscriptions recording sacrifices to Demokratia in 332/1 and 331/0 indicate that she had an Athenian cult in the late fourth century, and a statue of Demokratia may have stood on a base dedicated to her by the boule in 333/2. The figures in the relief of the antityranny law are not identified by labels, but Demos conforms closely to his known type, and both figures must refer, in the usual manner of figures in document reliefs, to the specific content of the accompanying inscription.

Figure 3: *Demos, left, Athena, and Herakles, probably honoring a figure on the lost left half of the relief. Athens, National Archaeological Museum 2407. Photograph courtesy National Archaeological Museum.*

The appearance of personifications of Athenian democracy and its institutions in public reliefs in the fourth century can be attributed to a combination of artistic and political factors. Beginning in the late fifth century and throughout the fourth century, the use of personifications in Athenian art became more frequent and complex, encouraged by an intellectual climate that appreciated abstraction in literature and art. The source of many of the personifications was no longer poetry but prose, specifically the writings of philosophers like Plato, whose famous passage in the *Krito* has Sokrates arguing with the lifelike Laws, or the speeches and writings of the orators, whose personification of both abstract and concrete terms was an important part of their language of persuasion. At the same time, throughout the course of the fourth century, Athenian democracy became increasingly specialized. In the interest of greater efficiency, new officials were added, and greater consistency was expected in secretarial, financial, and legal matters. With greater professionalism came increased self-consciousness and a preoccupation with democracy, which must have been fueled by the critical examination of various forms of constitution so popular with contemporary philosophers and orators, and by the very real external and internal threats to Athenian democracy to which the anti-tyranny law is eloquent testimony. The result was that, while Athena continued to appear in document reliefs of the fourth century, she was often pushed aside by figures who represented aspects of Athenian democracy, a revealing shift that illustrates how far the Athenian democrats of the fourth century, in their official art at least, had come to identify themselves with their constitution.

For permission to publish the document reliefs discussed here, I am grateful to G. Dontas, former Ephor of the Acropolis: D. Peppa-Delmouzou, Director of the Epigraphical Museum; T. Leslie Shear, Jr., Field Director of the Agora Excavations; and N. Yalouris, former Director of the National Archaeological Museum.

## SUGGESTED READING

R. Hinks, *Myth and Allegory in Ancient Art*, London 1939

J. J. Pollitt, *Art and Experience in Classical Greece*, Cambridge 1972

P. J. Rhodes, "Athenian Democracy after 403 B.C.," *Classical Journal* 75 (1979) 303-323

A. Shapiro, "The Origins of Allegory in Greek Art," *Boreas* 9 (1986) 4-23

# THE BIRTH OF DEMOCRACY

## PETER G. CALLIGAS
### DIRECTOR OF THE "A" EPHOREIA
### OF PREHISTORIC AND CLASSICAL ANTIQUITIES

In the words of Aristotle, the human being is a "social animal." Humans have a natural desire to live in groups, and just as in the natural kingdom, these groups require a form of internal organization that will reflect the group's particular rules of co-existence and allocate roles to members, so as best to meet the group's basic needs for food and shelter, as well as offer protection from outside enemies, whether animals or fellow human beings. Unlike the other species of social animals however, humans have developed a variety of very different forms of internal organizations, different types of government, which in each case express the development and progress attained by a particular group and the state of human relations within it.

The achievements of the large authoritarian states of the East and the mighty kingdoms of Minoan and Mycenaean Greece attest to the potential of centralized power in prehistoric times. There, a small number of individuals remained in possession of political as well as material power, while the mass of the population was in a state of servitude to those few. But the Greeks of historical times developed another form of government in which a greater number of people participated on a more equitable basis, and the power of the few was gradually restricted. To this type of government, which allowed for the development of individual freedom and creativity, the Greeks gave the name of "the power [*kratos*] of the many [*tou demou*]," i.e. "democracy."

However, this type of Greek government was a difficult one to achieve and establish, requiring heavy sacrifices and going through numerous, albeit comparatively short, stages of development, until it triumphed in fifth-century Athens. Although the particular historical factors which had converged to enable the Athenian democracy to blossom later gave their place to other circumstances alien to it, its achievements remained a focal point and its ideas a source of inspiration for subsequent societies, even to the present day.

After a long period of dispersed habitation and patriarchal social organization during the tenth and ninth centuries B.C., and for reasons that are still not clear to us, the Greeks of historical times were compelled around 800 B.C. to restructure their existence and urbanize. The development of new, small, and fortified settlements is characteristic of many regions of insular and continental Greece in this period and attests to the assembly of the previously dispersed inhabitants within a common protected area. This move created new needs for the inhabitants which were expressed with the development of a common—and communal—political, social, and religious life.

On the other hand, the extensive geographical partition of the Greek landscape led to the dispersion of the inhabitants into small regional groups. And so, from these small fortified settlements, there developed the numerous city-states of ancient Greece, each based within a fortified town and extending its power to the surrounding countryside.

The countryside was of vital importance to the city-state, supplying it with food and, particularly in areas such as Attica, playing a decisive role in the development of political affairs. Already by as early as tne middle of the seventh century B.C., literary sources (Aristotle, *Constitution of Athens* II, 1-2) reveal that in the beginning of the Athenian state, almost all the land of Attica belonged to a few individuals, the "notables" or nobles. The "masses," the people, rented the land, which they cultivated, but were forced into slavery if they were unable to meet their obligations toward the landowners. This potentially explosive and highly irregular situation was both generated and aggravated by the excesses of the aristocratic regime, while the intense social unrest and confrontation it inevitably caused culminated, following Cylon's unsuccessful revolt (640-630 B.C.), with the exile of the opposing Athenian clan of the Alkmaeonids. It became obvious that certain issues needed to be addressed and the land-owning nobility attempted to resolve the situation by imposing a written code of laws.

The task was entrusted to the Athenian Draco (621 B.C.), who thus became the first law-maker of Attica, codifying the institutions of the young state. He divided the free citizens into three classes according to their economic power (*pentakosio-medimnoi, hippeis,* and *zeugitai*), strengthened the existing aristocratic form of government, and established heavy penalties for those who broke his laws. As Draco's legislation did not fundamentally alter social inequity it also failed to impose harmony between the classes. Matters in fact became worse, as violent unrest and strife between the few and the many continued. Solon, who was himself from a noble Athenian family and *archon* of the year in 594/3 B.C., was called

upon to remedy this volatile situation.

Solon brought into immediate implementation a system of legal measures which became known as the *seisachtheia*, meaning the removal or lifting of a heavy load, or burden. It involved the cancellation of debts, the abolition of borrowing on the security of the debtor's person, and the liberation of those who had already been sold into slavery because of debt, both in and outside of Athens.

There followed a reorganization of the system of government along more egalitarian principles. Among other similarly far-reaching measures, the fourth and poorest class of citizens, the *thetes*, were admitted into the Assembly of the People. A second Council was established, consisting of four hundred members, taken equally from the four tribes into which the Athenians were traditionally divided. Popular courts of justice were founded while Solon also provided for the economic amelioration of the weaker members of society, took measures for the improvement of crop yields, and introduced a new standardization of the weights and measures then in use. It should be noted that the first Attic coins, the silver staters, based on new metric standards, were brought into circulation only a few years later, while the arts of pottery and vase-painting flourished to such an extent that Attic products soon superseded Corinthian ones in the markets abroad.

It is hardly surprising that Solon's reforms initially met with considerable opposition, but they were finally accepted and firmly consolidated. They became the foundation of the Athenian form of government that attained its fullest and most democratic expression in the fifth century B.C. The years that followed Solon's legislative work also saw the emergence of political parties in

Athens, along lines that reflected the socio-economic stratification of the state in three distinct ideological tendencies. The *Paralioi* were the people of the coast-land, the seamen and ship-owners who favored a moderate political regime; the *Pediakoi*, the inhabitants of the plains, were the nobles and wealthy landowners who desired an oligarchy; and finally the *Diakrioi*, or "people from the hills," were the inhabitants of the poorer regions and the herdsmen, who supported a democracy.

The leader of the third faction, the democrats, was Peisistratos who nevertheless aspired and finally succeeded in establishing his own personal power over the city. With the aid of mercenary soldiers, he managed to override the institutions established by Solon and install a tyrannical government. Although many great achievements mark his long and turbulent reign—he died in 527 B.C.—political thought stagnated and its development was arrested. Particularly during the rule of his sons and successors, the regime became increasingly tyrannical and provoked popular discontent.

When one of the Peisistratids, Hipparchos, was murdered in 514 B.C. by the nobles Harmodios and Aristogeiton, the Athenians worshipped the two tyrannicides as heroes, reserving for them quite exceptional posthumous honors such as annual sacrifices and the erection of statues.

The tyranny finally came to an end in 511/10 B.C. with the expulsion of the remaining Peisistratid, Hippias, but this only marked the beginning of a fresh bitter struggle between the oligarchs under Isagoras, and the democrats led by Kleisthenes. The political system was not yet strong enough to impose its institutions on the warring factions and contain their struggle within them.

And it was amid great difficulties that in 508/7

B.C.—approximately two thousand and five hundred years ago—Kleisthenes contrived to secure the vote of the Assembly of the People in favor of his reform proposals, which were aimed at restricting the strength of the oligarchs and broadening the popular base of the democrats. By dividing Attica into demes and increasing the number of tribes to ten, Kleisthenes restructured and expanded the citizen body. The city's military forces were reconstituted on a similar basis and a new Council, of the Five Hundred, was established to wield wider authority and replace Solon's Council of Four Hundred. The authority of the eponymous *archon* was notably curtailed, while a variety of measures aimed at protecting the democratic political system against the threat of a new tyranny were established. It was within this context that the law on ostracism was introduced, although it was not actually enforced until later. This law provided for the banishment of any individual who was suspected of subverting the democratic regime or was considered to pose a danger to it, and took its name from the inscribed potsherds (*ostraka*) with which the popular verdict against someone was expressed.

Kleisthenes' reforms armed the people of Athens, the Athenian *demos*, with substantial power as well as strength, secured the equality of all free citizens before the law, and paved the way for the democratic conquests of the fifth century B.C. under Themistokles, Ephialtes, and Perikles. As the powerful demos of the free Athenians turned toward the sea and built up its navy, it was able to confront the Persian invaders victoriously at Marathon (490 B.C.), Salamis (480 B.C.), and Plataeae (479 B.C.) and safeguard its military achievements. And from within its powerful "wooden fortresses," the democratic city of Athens established the thalassocracy of the fifth century, which furnished it with enormous wealth, power, and creative impetus.

Athens had struggled long and made painful sacrifices to establish a government that sought to be guided by the will of the many as opposed to the arbitrary desire of the few. And the city proudly exhibited its artistic creations and its intellectual contribution to ancient poetry, tragedy, and philosophy, as a celebration of its own greatness and a testimony to the high morale of its free and democratic citizens. The Athenians of the fifth century felt they had achieved the "power of the many," and although the next 2,500 years brought many additional elements to our concept of democracy, the ideals expressed then continue to illuminate our way and inspire our quest.

# POTTERY, PRIVATE LIFE, AND POLITICS IN DEMOCRATIC ATHENS

## ALAN SHAPIRO
### STEVENS INSTITUTE OF TECHNOLOGY

In 508 B.C., as Kleisthenes was carrying out his pioneering work of creating a democracy for Athens, the city's potters' quarter could boast its own brand of "Pioneers." This is the nickname coined by Sir John Beazley, the great scholar of Greek vase-painting, for a small group of artists who, in the years about 520-500, brought about radical changes in an art form with a centuries-old tradition in Athens. In addition to the more technical achievements that those men pioneered in vase shapes, coloration, and draughtsmanship, there is another way in which they were particularly innovative. From their vantage point in the heart of the Archaic city, they were keen observers of every stratum of society, from the aristocracy to the humblest slaves, and they have given us some of our most vivid pictures of Athenian life.

Because the Pioneers were the finest potters and painters of their generation, their patrons were often leading aristocrats, and one of their favorite subjects was that quintessentially aristocratic institution, the *symposion* or drinking party (see Case 1). Indeed, most of their vases were made for use at a symposion: the large *kraters* for mixing wine and water, the cups and mugs for individual guests. No one captured the spirit of the symposion better than Euphronios, who is today the best known of the Pioneers (Figs. 1, 2).

Euphronios' symposion is in full swing (Fig. 1). Much wine has been consumed, and slave boys hurry to fetch more from a huge bowl depicted on the reverse (Fig. 2). Each of the two elaborate couches is shared by a male couple, one bearded, the other not. They represent the ideal relationship of older lover (*erastes*) and youthful beloved (*eromenos*) that in Athens was institutionalized among the social elite and celebrated in poetry and art. The couple at left, Theodemos and Melas, each carefully balance a very full cup of wine, while the couple at right is more intent on the music of a flute-girl named Syko (*Fig*). The youth, Smikros, reaches out to silence her instrument, perhaps because his companion, Ekphantides, has just burst into a spontaneous bit of song. The words that spill from his mouth—"O Apollo, to you and blessed [Artemis] . . . "—could come from a hymn by Anakreon, the East Greek poet most closely associated with the symposion milieu. Anakreon had come to Athens in 522 B.C., at the invitation of the tyrant Hipparchos, and caught the fancy of the aristocracy as well as the eye of the vase-painters.

Smikros, the youth in front of the flute-girl, must be the vase-painter of that name, a contemporary of Euphronios and a fellow Pioneer. He returned the compliment to Euphronios by depicting him on a wine-cooler (*psykter*) among young athletes and their admirers. Since there is no true portraiture, in the modern sense, in Attic vase-painting, such inscriptions naming friends and acquaintances may be a kind of "in joke" among

Figure 1: *Attic red-figure calyx-krater, Side A. Munich, Staatliche Antikensammlungen 8935. Ca. 510 B.C. Photo Christa Kopperman.*

Figure 2: *Side B of the krater, Figure 1.*

the painters who worked side by side and must often have competed for business. They also, however, provide evidence for a more serious point, often misunderstood: the openness and fluidity of Athenian society, the casual social interaction of men of different classes. Although the aristocracy retained prestige and influence in the early years of the democracy, this was no caste system with rigid separation of the social strata. Even the tyrant Peisistratos owed much of his popularity to his "common touch." And in the entrepreneurial atmosphere fostered by Solon's reforms, a potter or painter profitting from Athens' dominance in overseas markets could achieve considerable wealth and status. Expensive dedicatory statues were set up by several artisans on the Athenian Acropolis, including one by Euphronios himself.

The reverse side of Euphronios' krater (Fig. 2) contains an inscription in praise of a young Athenian man-about-town: "Leagros is handsome" (*Leagros kalos*). The custom of adding these so-called kalos inscriptions to vases goes back to the mid-sixth century but was most intensively practiced in the last years of the tyranny and the first decades of the democracy (*ca.* 520-450 B.C.). Although there is undeniably an erotic overtone (and occasionally women are also so praised), these inscriptions primarily are a celebration of prominent young aristocrats who frequented the potters' quarter and attracted the painter's eye. The persistence of kalos inscriptions is another testimony to the vigor of the aristocratic ethos in Athens under the democracy, at least down to the time of Perikles, when they somewhat abruptly disappear.

Because a young man's bloom of youth is of limited duration, and the chronology of Attic vases is quite precise, kalos inscriptions are an essential tool in reconstructing the careers of many known Athenians. For Leagros, for example, who is named more often than any other, we can posit a birth of about 530. Not long before the Persian invasion of 480 he dedicated a statue in the sanctuary of the Twelve Gods, located on the north side of the Agora. The statue is lost, but its inscribed base has survived. A red-figure cup shows a statue of a young athlete that may help us to visualize Leagros' dedication. Since the scene itself carries an inscription praising Leagros, it has been suggested that this represents the actual statue, admired by a now middleaged Leagros.

Leagros most likely fell in battle in 465 (Herodotus 9.75), but he left a son, Glaukon, who was almost as popular with the vase-painters of the 470's and 460's as his father had been with the Pioneers. Kalos inscriptions that include a patronymic (e.g., "Glaukon son of Leagros is handsome") are an added boon to the historian, for they help to fill in the genealogies of prominent Athenian families. In a few happy instances, we can correlate kalos inscriptions with *ostraka*, since it is quite possible that the same man famed for his beauty at eighteen was politically active (and dangerous) at forty.

Recent scholarship has reinforced the impression that no aspect of private, daily life in Athens escaped the scrutiny of the vase-painters. But this fascination is balanced by an almost complete lack of interest in depicting the public and civic life of the city. It is important to remember how many essential and familiar elements of Athenian life are *not* represented by the vase-painters: the *ekklesia* (citizen assembly); the *Boule* (council); the various magistrates and officials (*prytaneis*, *archons*, and *strategoi*, or generals); and the law-

Figure 3: Attic black-figure pelike. Naples, Museo Archaeologico Nazionale 3358. Ca. 520 B.C. Photo Deutsches Archäologisches Institut, Rome.

courts. The chief reason for the discrepancy is plain: Vase-painting is primarily a private art form, the objects themselves made for use in a domestic context, often the symposion, but also in the women's sphere and elsewhere in the household.

At best, we may occasionally catch glimpses of Athenian civic institutions in mythological guise. The most striking example is the story of the Arms

*Figure 4: Attic red-figure neck-amphora. Louvre G222. Ca. 470 B.C. Photo Réunion des Musées Nationaux.*

*Figure 5: Attic red-figure stamnos. London, British Museum E455. Ca. 440 B.C. Courtesy Trustees of the British Museum.*

of Achilles: the contest to determine which of the Greek heroes at Troy would receive the divine armor, forged for Achilles by the god Hephaistos, after the hero's death. The myth contained two key elements reminiscent of political practice in Athens: first, a rhetorical contest between the two principal contenders, Odysseus and Ajax, each making his argument for why he deserved the

arms; and second, a vote of the heroes to determine the award.

The speaking contest is depicted on a black-figure vase of the late sixth century (Fig. 3). Although the names of the heroes are inscribed and the armor for which they compete is prominently displayed, the men themselves could have stepped out of the Athenian ekklesia. Odysseus, the speaker, stands calmly on the *bema*, or speaker's platform, steadying himself with a long staff in one hand. The other arm is completely enveloped in the folds of his himation. This curious pose, making any kind of hand gestures impossible, seems unlikely for a public speaker, especially in the present-day Mediterranean, where hands can speak volumes. But in classical Athens, the calm, self-controlled demeanor of the speaker was highly prized, while the wildly gesticulating demagogue was often censured. We may compare the speaker depicted on an Early Classical vase (Fig. 4), standing atop a stepped platform. He too has both arms wrapped up in his cloak, to demonstrate his cool self-restraint. On the Naples vase (Fig 3), Ajax, waiting his turn to speak, assumes the pose of the attentive audience, leaning on a long staff (hallmark of the Athenian citizen in vase-painting, as in Fig. 4), legs casually crossed, left arm akimbo.

After the debate, the other heroes voted on who deserved the armor. When the Greek heroes cast their votes on red-figure vases (see Case 13.4), they used pebbles for ballots. Usually the pebbles were neatly stacked in the open, and the outcome was clear for all to see. The Athenians, however, favored the use of secret ballots, often casting their votes in bronze *hydrias*, or water jars.

If, as we have suggested, the public life of democratic Athens is generally absent from the repertoire of the vase-painters, one significant exception must be made for religious life, which in its many manifestations in cult ritual, sacrifice, and festivals was very much a public affair. Many of the scenes involve real Athenians, occasionally named in inscriptions, although mostly just "typical" men and women.

The centerpiece of Greek religious ritual was the blood sacrifice. A small oil jug (*lekythos*) depicts the victims, a pair of oxen, led by two youths. Ahead of them, an elaborately garbed woman carries on her head a *kanoun*, an offering tray that might hold, for example, barley to sprinkle on the animals. After the slaughter, pieces of meat were roasted on a spit for distribution to the worshippers (Fig. 5). Here a bearded man named Archenautes, no doubt a real Athenian of the time of Perikles, officiates and pours a libation on the altar from a *kylix*. A youth named Nikodemos

Figure 6: Attic red-figure amphora. Munich, Staatliche Antikensammlungen 2315. Ca. 480 B.C. Museum photo.

roasts the meat while a second stands ready and a flute-player provides musical accompaniment. This vase was made in the age of the Parthenon, when Athenian artists liked to ennoble, even heroize everyday life, with little touches like the "heroic nudity" of the two youths and the winged goddess Nike (Victory) hovering over the scene in a kind of divine epiphany.

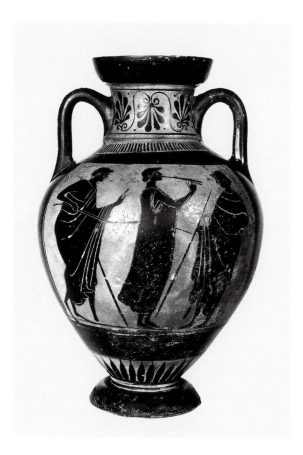

*Figure 7: Attic black-figure Panathenaic amphora, Side A. Manchester Museum III H 52. Photo Museum.*

*Figure 8: Side B of Figure 7.*

The gods and heroes of the Athenian state religion were each worshipped in different ways, some more publicly than others. The god Hermes, for example, patron of travelers (and thieves) was typically the object of solitary veneration at small roadside shrines in the Attic countryside, as were some of the heroes to whom the common man felt especially close. In one scene (Fig. 6), an Athe-

nian youth is on his way to make a dedication at a rustic sanctuary of the hero Herakles. The dedication consists of a small votive plaque bearing a likeness of the club-wielding hero that will be hung up in the sanctuary, along with a sprig of greenery to adorn it. The shape of the vase, which copies that of the Panathenaic prize *amphora*, suggests that our youth may be hoping for help from Herakles, the athletic hero par excellence, when he competes in the Games.

The major event of the Athenian religious calendar, in fact, was the Panathenaic festival, celebrating the birthday of the city goddess Athena. In the time of Perikles, the festival comprised not only large-scale sacrifices of oxen and the athletic games for which prize vases filled with oil were awarded but also contests for musicians and *rhapsodes* (reciters of Homeric poetry). The winners in these events received large cash prizes and were celebrated throughout Greece. Many vase-painters recorded their victories. One contestant, in the competition for solo flute-players (*auletes*), performs to a shorthand audience of two male listeners (Fig. 8). The vase is a miniature version of the big prize vases given to victorious athletes, perhaps made as a souvenir for the winner or his family. Although the striding Athena on the front (Fig. 7) is like the goddess on the prize vases, the columns that flank her are not topped by the conventional fighting cocks. Instead, the round objects may represent bronze mixing bowls (*lebetes*), a traditional heroic prize since the time of Homer. In these years, with the Athenian Empire at its height, the Panathenaia was the most visible symbol of democratic Athens' success and attracted visitors and competitors from all over the Greek world.

SUGGESTED READING

J. Frel, "Euphronios and His Fellows," in *Ancient Greek Art and Iconography*, ed. Warren G. Moon, Madison 1983, 147-158

M. L. Lang and M. Crosby, *Agora X, Weights, Measures and Tokens*, Princeton 1964

A. E. Raubitschek, "Leagros," *Hesperia* 8 (1939) 155-164

D. M. Robinson and E. J. Fluck, *A Study of the Greek Love Names*, Baltimore 1937

A. Shapiro, "Kalos Inscriptions with Patronymic," *Zeitschrift für Papyrologie und Epigraphik* 57 (1987) 107-118

E. Simon, *Festivals of Attica*, Madison 1983

E. T. Vermeule, "Fragments of a Symposion by Euphronios," *Antike Kunst* 8 (1965) 34-39

# EXHIBITION CATALOGUE

### DIANA BUITRON-OLIVER
### AND
### JOHN McK. CAMP II

# INTRODUCTION TO THE EXHIBITION

Classical Athens saw the rise of an achievement unparalleled in history. Perikles, Aischylos, Sophokles, Plato, Demosthenes, and Praxiteles represent just a few of the statesmen and philosophers, playwrights and orators, historians and artists who flourished there in the 5th and 4th centuries B.C., when Athens numbered among the most powerful and influential city-states in Greece. Collectively they were responsible for sowing the seeds of Western civilization. Of the many gifts passed down to us by the Athenians, including philosophy, theater, painting, sculpture, and architecture, none is more significant than their chosen form of government: democracy, rule by the people. Indeed, it can be convincingly argued that all the other achievements depended first on how the city was governed, on the open and free society that respected the dignity, rights, and aspirations of the individual.

In looking back over time to find and understand the origins of our own democratic way of life, we can go back to Athens at the end of the 6th century B.C. and no further. The year 1993 represents the 2,500th anniversary of this extraordinary innovation. Greek democracy was fostered and encouraged by several statesmen whose names and careers are fairly well known: Solon, Themistokles, and Perikles. The revolutionary events of 508/7 B.C., however, were sparked by a man whose name is recognized by few today: Kleisthenes. Member of a powerful aristocratic family, he remains a shadowy historical figure, known only from a handful of references in Aristotle and Herodotos. Yet his reforms of the constitution put the Athenians irrevocably on the road to democracy.

The exhibition for which this catalogue is a record is intended to illustrate and tell the story of the development of democracy in Athens. Most of the material comes from the excavations of the Athe-

*Rotunda, National Archives Building, Washington, D.C.*

nian Agora, carried out by the American School of Classical Studies at Athens from 1931 until today. A large open square, surrounded on all four sides by public buildings, the Agora was in every respect the center of town. The excavation of buildings, monuments, and small objects has illustrated the important role it played in all aspects of civic life. The senate chamber, public office buildings, and archives have been excavated. The lawcourts are represented by the discovery of bronze ballots and a waterclock. Long colonnades (stoas) provided shaded walkways for those discussing business, politics, and philosophy, while statues and commemorative monuments reminded citizens of former triumphs. Administrative, political, judicial, commercial, social, cultural, and religious activities all found a place here together in the heart of ancient Athens. In modern terms it would be the village green of a traditional American town, or, on a large scale, the Mall in Washington, D.C.

A comparison of the Agora to modern civic centers leads us to consider the extraordinary similarities between our own times and then. The Athenian government, too, was divided into three branches, executive, judiciary, and legislative, with authority divided among them. To be sure, there were many obvious differences between ancient and modern democracy and the societies that created them, but the parallels are enlightening, and this catalogue will draw attention to them when appropriate. An effort has also been made to allow the ancient Athenians to speak for themselves. Numerous quotes from ancient authors explain the material included as well as the workings of Athenian democracy. The ancient Athenians also speak to us through their painted vases, which represent scenes of daily life under the democracy, and refer more obliquely to the workings of Athenian government through new ways of representing mythological stories.

# FREE STANDING OBJECTS IN ROTUNDA
## BUSTS OF PERIKLES AND DEMOSTHENES

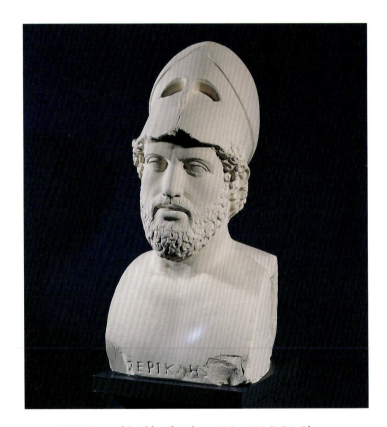

*00.01 Bust of Perikles (lived ca. 500–429 B.C.). Plaster cast after a bust in the British Museum, London. Museum of Art and Archaeology, University of Missouri—Columbia.*

This great statesman of classical Athens was responsible for building the Parthenon and other monuments on the Acropolis. His speech honoring the Athenians who fell in the first year of the Peloponnesian war provided an eloquent description of democracy.

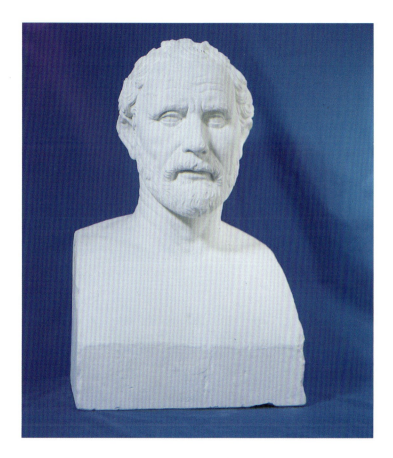

*00.02 Bust of Demosthenes (lived ca. 384—322 B.C.).
Plaster cast after a bust in the Glyptothek, Munich.
From the H. W. Sage Collection of Classical Sculpture at Cornell University, Ithaca, New York.*

In stirring speeches, this political leader urged the Athenians to live up to their democratic ideals of equality and liberty.

# MODELS OF THE ATHENIAN AGORA

Around the sides of this great square the Athenians built most of their civic buildings; hence the Agora became the center of the Athenian democracy. Here were to be found the senate building, the central archives, the chief magistrates' offices, the military headquarters of both army and navy, the lawcourts, and the mint.

These buildings were built and rebuilt over the course of the eight hundred years during which the Agora served as the civic center of Athens. The models depict the area at two of its most important periods:

*00.03A The Athenian Agora c. 500 B.C. Model by Petros Demetriades and Kostas Papoulias, Athens, Agora Museum.*

The Agora seems to have been laid out as a public area late in the 6th century B.C., presumably under the tyrant Peisistratos and his sons. In 500 B.C., soon after the Kleisthenic reforms, new buildings were added. Most important, perhaps, was the *Bouleuterion* (Senate House), where the newly created senate of 500 members representing the ten "tribes" of Athens met most days to consider legislation for the city. Also built at about the same time was the Royal Stoa which housed the offices of the king archon, the official in charge of religious matters and the laws.

*00.03B The Athenian Agora c. 400 B.C. Model by Petros Demetriades and Kostas Papoulias, Athens, Agora Museum.*

The 5th century B.C. saw the rise of Athens to a position of extraordinary prominence. During this century the Athenians fought and defeated the Persians, refined their democratic system under the leadership of Perikles, and built the great temples on the Acropolis. The last decades of the century saw them engaged in a terrible and costly war with Sparta, a war that was the democracy's harshest test. The model of the Agora in 400 B.C. shows the civic center at a time when Athens had provided herself with all the public buildings necessary for the functioning of the fully developed democratic system. The buildings shown on the model served in one form or another for the next several generations.

# MARBLE STELE RECORDING A LAW
# AGAINST TYRANNY

In 338 B.C. Philip II of Macedon and his son Alexander defeated the Athenians and other Greek states in a battle at Chaironeia in central Greece. In the following year (337/6 B.C.) the Athenians passed a law against tyranny that reflects Athenian uncertainty concerning the future of their democracy. The decree was written up on a marble stele capped with a handsome relief showing Democracy crowning the seated Demos (people) of Athens. In the exhibition is displayed a copy of the original. The text of the decree reads:

In the archonship of Phrynichos, in the ninth prytany of Leontis for which Chairestratos, son of Ameinias, of Acharnai, was secretary; Menestratos of Aixone, of the proedroi, put the question to a vote; Eukrates, son of Aristodimos, of Peiraeus, made the motion; with Good Fortune of the Demos of the Athenians, be it resolved by the Nomothetai [lawgivers]: If anyone should rise up against the Demos for tyranny or join in establishing the tyranny or overthrow the Demos of the Athenians

or the democracy in Athens, whoever kills him who does any of these things shall be blameless. It shall not be permitted for anyone of the Councillors of the Council from the Areopagos [Supreme Court]—if the Demos or the democracy in Athens having been overthrown—to go up into the Areopagos or sit in the Council or deliberate about anything. If anyone of the Councillors of the Areopagos—the Demos or the democracy in Athens having been overthrown—goes up into the Areopagos or sits in the Council or deliberates about anything, both he and his progeny shall be deprived of civil rights and his substance shall be confiscated and a tenth given to the Goddess. The secretary of the Council shall inscribe this law on two stelai of stone and set one of them by the entrance into the Areopagos, that entrance, namely, near where one goes into the Bouleuterion, and the other in the Ekklesia. For the inscribing of the stelai the treasurer of the Demos shall give 20 drachmas from the moneys expendable by the Demos according to decrees.

*00.04 Stele with a relief showing Democracy crowning Demos (the people of Athens). Plaster cast of the marble original, ca. 337 B.C. Athens, Agora Museum, I 6524.*

The inscription is an Athenian law forbidding cooperation with those plotting an antidemocratic coup and calling for the acquittal of anyone accused of murdering the tyrant. As the text explains, Eukrates made the motion, and the question was put to a vote in the archonship of Phrynichos. The law was inscribed on two *stelai* (stone markers) to be set up at the entrances of the Bouleuterion (senate house) and the *ekklesia* (assembly).

# ATHENS BEFORE DEMOCRACY

## CASES 1–4

# 1

## THE ATHENIAN ARISTOCRACY

Before democracy, from the 8th to the 6th century B.C., Athens was prosperous economically but no more significant than many other city-states in Greece. Silver deposits south of Athens, quarries of fine white marble, and extensive clay beds that skilled potters used to good advantage made the city wealthy but otherwise unremarkable. As in other Greek cities, political power was in the hands of several large aristocratic families or clans (*genei*) which controlled large areas of Attica, the territory around Athens. Social prestige and political office were linked to property and military prowess, and most of the population had virtually no role in the political life of the city. Aristotle describes the situation in the 7th century B.C. as follows:

> Appointment to the supreme offices of state went by birth and wealth; and they were held at first for life, and afterwards for a term of ten years. (*Athenian Constitution* 3.1)

At times these aristocratic families ruled in relative harmony; on occasion competition and strife between them was severe. Until the 6th century, Athens and her aristocratic political system were typical of many Greek city-states.

These aristocratic families enjoyed considerable wealth and contacts with aristocrats elsewhere. Painted pottery (1.3 and 1.4) and surviving fragments of poetry depict the aristocracy at play, usually reclining comfortably at a drinking party or *symposion*. Material wealth was displayed in the form of costly dedications made in sanctuaries such as the Acropolis of Athens or at Brauron, Eleusis, and Sounion. Cemeteries also provide rich material from this period: lavish burials contained intricately worked gold jewelry (1.1) and unusual glass objects (1.2), along with specially made funerary vases (2.1). By the 6th century the grave was often marked by a handsome marble statue of a *kouros* (nude youth) or a *kore* (finely dressed maiden). In later, democratic times, such ostentatious displays of funerary luxury were sharply curtailed:

> On account of the enormous size of the tombs that we now see in the *Kerameikos* (cemetery), it was provided by law that no one should build one that required more than three days work for ten men. Nor was it permitted to adorn a tomb with stucco-work nor to place upon it herms, as they are called (Cicero, *De legibus* 2.26.64).

*1.1,2 Jewelry from the grave of a woman, about 850 B.C.*

The jewelry was found in the Athenian Agora in a cremation burial of the mid-9th century B.C., a time when the area was used as a cemetery. Grave offerings included, besides the jewelry, a number of vases decorated in the Geometric style, which flourished in the 9th and 8th centuries. Among them was an unusual model of a granary and a large amphora (two-handled pot) that contained the bones and ashes of the deceased.

*1.1 Pair of gold earrings. L.: 0.065 m. Athens, Agora Museum J 148.*

Gold jewelry was unusual in 9th-century Greece. Each earring consists of a shaft made of fine wires to which is attached a trapezoidal plaque decorated with filigree and granulation. Three pomegranate finials hang from the bottom of the plaque. The earrings would have been suspended from a thin gold wire or hook passed through the ears.

*1.2 Necklace of glass and faience beads. Max. L. of the largest bead: 0.047 m.; min. L.: 0.004 m. Athens, Agora Museum G 587-591, J 149.*

The elements of the necklace include glass and faience beads that were found together in the burial. They have been restrung to recreate the original appearance of the necklace.

*Athenian (Attic) red-figure kylix (drinking cup), early 5th century B.C.; H.: 0.075 m. Athens, National Archaeological Museum 1357.*

At the symposion, participants often ended the evening with singing. The banqueter in this picture has thrown back his head in the customary position for singing. He caresses a hare, a common gift between lovers. The red-figure technique, which reverses the black-figure scheme and leaves the figures in the natural red of the clay on a black background, was invented around 525 B.C. and quickly superseded the older technique for most vases.

*1.3 Athenian (Attic) black-figure olpe (jug), 540-530 B.C. Attributed to the Amasis Painter. H.: 0.26 m. Athens, Agora Museum P 24673.*

This fragmentary clay jug shows a symposion with banqueters reclining on a couch, a typically aristocratic activity. On the left a girl plays the double pipes (*auloi*), providing music for the occasion, and on the right stands a youth. A low table spread with fruit and meat has been placed in front of the couch. The vase is decorated in the black-figure technique in which the figures are rendered in black on the natural red clay surface of the vase; details are done by incision through the black, or with red and white colors.

*1.5 Photograph of a statue of a youth (kouros): Kroisos. H.: 1.94 m. Athens, National Archaeological Museum 3851.*

Aristocratic families commemorated their deceased sons with statues. This figure was found at Anavysos, in Attica, and is often called the Anavysos Kouros. His name, Kroisos, is known from the inscription on the base of the statue: "Stay and mourn at the monument of dead Kroisos whom furious Ares destroyed one day as he fought in the front ranks."

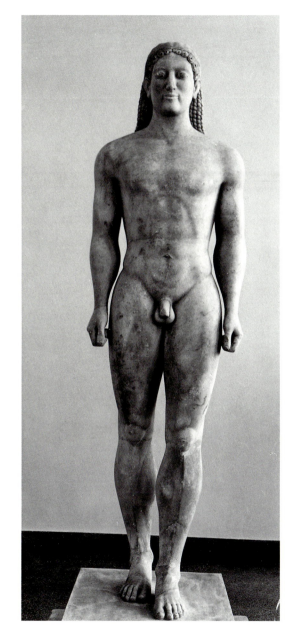

# 2

## SOLON THE LAWGIVER

By the early 6th century B.C. social tensions in Athens had become acute, pitting the poorer citizens against rich and powerful landowners. Many citizens were reduced to the status of share croppers, and others had actually sold themselves into slavery to meet their debts. To resolve the crisis the Athenians appointed Solon as *archon* (magistrate) to serve as mediator and lawgiver. Plutarch and Aristotle describe in some detail the constitution devised by Solon, who then went into voluntary exile to avoid being pressured into amending this legislation.

Solon canceled most debts and freed those Athenians who had been enslaved, but he refused to redistribute property or to deprive the aristocracy of most of the political power. As he tells us in his own words:

For to the common people I gave as
much power as is sufficient,
Neither robbing them of dignity, nor giving
them too much;
and those who had power, and were
marvelously rich,
Even for those I contrived that they
suffered no harm.
I stood with a mighty shield in
front of both classes,
and allowed neither of them to
prevail unjustly. (Plutarch, *Life of Solon* 18.4)

Solon's new constitution was based on ownership of property. This notion of political rights or citizenship depending on property is one found in many societies until relatively recent times. All the people were divided into four classes, and political power was distributed among them.

1. The *pentekosiomedimnoi*, those whose land produced at least 500 *medimnoi* (measures) of grain a year (2.1) which equals 730 bushels. These were eligible for the highest offices.

2. The *hippeis* (knights), those who could afford the expense of maintaining a horse (2.2) and whose property produced 300 medimnoi a year.

3. The *zeugitai* (teamsters), those who maintained a pair of oxen for plowing and whose land produced 200 medimnoi a year (2.3).

4. The *thetes* or common laborers (2.4).

All other native-born citizens now possessed an important and basic right: they could not be enslaved by their fellow citizens. As early as the time of Homer, to be a thete was regarded as only just above a slave: "I would rather follow the plow as thete to another man, one with no land allotted to him and not much to live on, than be King over all the perished dead" (*Odyssey* 2.489-491). Members of this lowest class were not allowed to hold office, but were given the right to sit and vote in the assembly and to sit as jurors in the law-courts. Over time this last right became exceedingly important (Cases 10-13).

An important concept clearly laid out for the first time in Solon's political poetry is the notion that political participation was the duty of the citizen, not just a privilege to be exercised or not as one chose:

> He saw that the state was often in a condition of factional strife, while some of the citizens were content to let things slide; he laid down a special law to deal with them, enacting that whoever when civil strife prevailed did not join forces with either party was to be disenfranchised and not to be a member of the state. (*Athenian Constitution* 8.5).

While Solonian reforms did not establish democracy, they were a crucial step on the Athenian road to democracy. Solon's constitution, consisting of moderate redistribution rather than a revolutionary transfer of political power, nonetheless granted important rights to the lowest class of citizens.

This middle course pleased no one, as he himself tells us:

> Wherefore I stood at guard on every side,
> A wolf at bay among a pack of hounds
> (*Athenian Constitution* 12.4).

Within a generation of Solon's reforms, factional strife among the powerful families led Athens once again to the brink of civil war, setting the stage for the next phase of Athenian political development.

*2.1 Athenian (Attic) Geometric chest with five model
"granaries" on the lid, mid-9th century B.C. H.: 0.253
m. Athens, Agora Museum P 27646.*

This unusual chest comes from the same burial as the
jewelry described earlier (1.1,2). The five cone-shaped
objects on the lid have been identified as model
granaries and may refer to the woman's status as a
member of the highest class, the landed aristocracy
designated by Solon pentekosiomedimnoi, whose land
produced 500 medimnoi (measures). Each of the five
granaries would thus represent 100 medimnoi. Both the
chest and the granaries are decorated with meander
patterns, a favorite Geometric ornament.

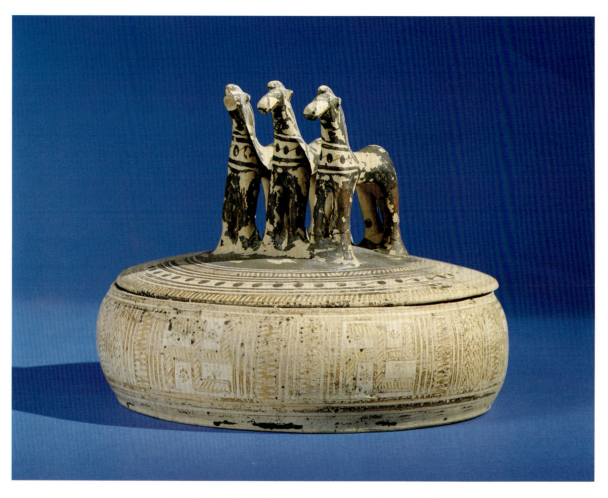

*2.2 Athenian (Attic) Geometric horse pyxis (box), mid-8th century B.C. H.: 0.16 m. Athens, Agora Museum P 5061.*

This round box has three horses on the lid. Ownership of horses required a certain degree of wealth and allowed the man who owned them to assume a role in defending the city as a member of a fighting cavalry, the knights. Thus, horses became a status symbol and sign of wealth.

*2.3 Terracotta figure of a pair of oxen driven by a man, 6th century B.C. H.: 0.10 m. Athens, National Archaeological Museum 18876.*

This image stands for Solon's third class of citizens, the zeugitai, who could maintain a pair of oxen for plowing and who served as heavy-armed infantrymen in time of war.

*2.4 Iron pick, date uncertain. Preserved L.: 0.127 m. Athens, Agora Museum IL 1287.*

Such a pick might have been used by a member of Solon's lowest class, the thetes, or common laborers.

2.5 *Photograph of vases from the cremation burial of a wealthy woman (1.1), including the chest with model granaries shown. Athens, Agora excavations.*

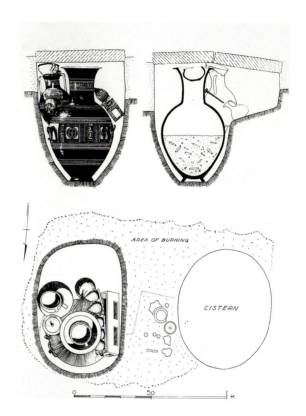

2.6 *Drawing of the cremation burial of a wealthy woman. Drawing by W. B. Dinsmoor, Jr.*

The bones and ashes were found in the large pot along with the gold jewelry and faience necklace displayed in Case 1. The other vessels, including the chest with model granaries, were placed around the large pot as grave offerings. The drawing shows side and top views of the burial.

# 3

## TYRANNY

As happened in many other Greek states, a tyrant arose in Athens in the 6th century B.C. His name was Peisistratos, and after several unsuccessful attempts he seized power in 546 B.C. and ruled until his death in 527, after which he was succeeded by his two sons, Hippias and Hipparchos.

Such tyrannies were a common feature of Greek political life as states made the transition from an aristocracy to either a democracy or an oligarchy. The Greek word τύραννος indicates that the individual seized or held power unconstitutionally but does not necessarily carry the negative force the word has today. Often the tyrant arose as the champion of the common people against the aristocracy. Peisistratos, head of one of the large aristocratic families, seized power by force during a period of factional strife. Though many Athenians fled or were forced into exile (Herodotus 1.64), Aristotle's assessment of his tenure is positive:

> Peisistratos' administration of the state was, as has been said, moderate, and more constitutional than tyrannic; he was kindly and mild in everything, and in particular he was merciful to offenders and moreover he advanced loans of money to the poor for their industries. (*Athenian Constitution* 16.1-2)

That Peisistratid rule was surprisingly open is borne out by a fragment of a list of archons (3.1) which shows that in 524 B.C.the future founder of democracy, Kleisthenes himself, held the chief magistracy while the tyrants were still in power, as did another rival aristocrat, Miltiades. For 522/1 B.C. we can read the name of the younger Peisistratos, grandson of the founder of the tyranny. Aristotle has further praise for the tyrants, at least in their early days:

> And in all other matters too he gave the multitude no trouble during his rule but always worked for peace and safeguarded tranquility; so that men were often to be heard saying that the tyranny of Peisistratos was the Golden Age of Kronos; for it came about later when his son succeeded him that the government became much harsher. And the greatest of all the things said of him was that he was popular and kindly in temper. For he was willing to administer everything according to the laws in all matters, never giving himself any advantage. …Both the notables and the men of the people were most of them willing for him to govern, since he won over the former by his hospitality and the latter by his assistance in their private affairs and was good-natured to both. (*Athenian Constitution* 16.7-9)

His reign, like that of so many tyrants, was characterized by large public works projects, the first in Athens for centuries. Large temples and altars were constructed for Zeus Olympios, Apollo Pythios, and the Twelve Gods (3.4). In addition, an extensive system of aqueducts and fountainhouses brought a reliable supply of good clean water into the city. The impact of this fine new water system is reflected in the fountainhouse scenes painted on dozens of black-figure hydrias (water jars) and other pots in the late 6th century (3.2). Matters changed with the death of Peisistratos when his two sons Hippias and Hip-parchos took over in 527 B.C. Aristotle describes the characters of the two brothers:

> Affairs were now under the authority of Hipparchos and Hippias, owing to their station and their ages, but the government was controlled by Hippias, who was the elder and was statesmanlike and wise by nature; whereas Hipparchos was fond of amusement and lovemaking and had literary tastes; it was he who brought to Athens the poets such as Anakreon and Simonides, and the others. (*Athenian Constitution* 18.1)

This transformation of Athens into a great cultural center is reflected in scenes on painted pottery of the period depicting the Ionian poet Anakreon, known for extravagance and sensuality (3.3).

*3.1 Fragment of an inscription, about 425 B.C. H.: 0.15 m.
W.: 0.195 m. Athens, Agora Museum I 4120.*

Broken from a large marble block inscribed with a list
of archons of Athens, this piece preserves parts of the
names of six archons of the 520's B.C.; two of them are
members of the family of Peisistratos: In the second line
we read Hippias, his son, and in the last line,
Peisistratos the younger, his grandson. The inscription
also records the names of two other well-known politicians active in the late 6th century B.C.: Miltiades,
future hero of the battle of Marathon against the Persians, and Kleisthenes, later to be the initiator of
democratic reforms. The letter forms date the inscription to the later part of the 5th century B.C., which
means the piece shown here recorded the names of
individuals who held office a century earlier.

*3.3 Athenian (Attic) white-ground, black-figure kyathos
(ladle), 520-500 B.C. H.: 0.09 m. Malibu, J. Paul
Getty Museum 77.AE.102, 78.AE.5.*

The tyrant Hipparchos was responsible for bringing
several poets of note to the Athenian court, among
them the Ionian poet Anakreon with whom the figure
on this vase is associated. The figure stands between
two large eyes, which are only partly preserved. He
holds a musical instrument, a kind of lyre (*barbiton*),
and wears an unusual costume consisting of a short
chiton, soft red boots, and a *mitra*, a turban-like head
covering from which his hair projects at the crown. This
style of dress has been associated with Anakreon's stay
in Athens. The vase could well have been used as a
ladle to serve wine at a symposion. The high handle
has been broken and is partly missing.

49

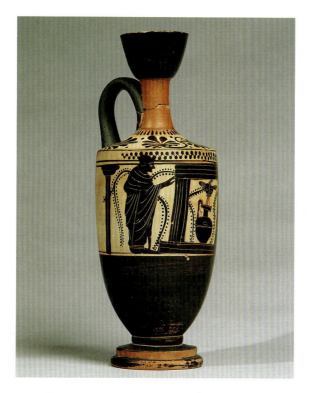

*3.2 Athenian (Attic) white-ground, black-figure lekythos (oil container), about 500 B.C. Attributed to the Gela Painter. H.: 0.265 m. Athens, Agora Museum P 24106.*

Building fountainhouses and thus improving the water supply of the city was one of several civic works initiated under the Peisistratid tyranny. In the picture on this vase, water gushes from a spout shaped like the head of a panther into the water jar (hydria) below. A woman waits for it to fill while another woman goes off with her jar full. The fountainhouse shown here is small, but we know of one fountainhouse built at this time that had nine waterspouts, the Enneakrounos, a building that has not so far been located by archaeologists. As this picture suggests, fountainhouses became meeting places for women whose otherwise circumscribed lives allowed them few such opportunities.

*3.4 Model of the Altar of the Twelve Gods. Model by Petros Demetriades and Kostas Papoulias, Athens, Agora Museum.*

Literary sources tell us that the younger Peisistratos, grandson of the founder of the tyranny, dedicated the Altar of the Twelve Gods when he was archon in 522/1 B.C. This monument was near the middle of the Agora square, the actual center of Athens, and was the point from which distances from Athens were measured. The altar was famous in antiquity as a place of asylum and refuge. No traces remain of the altar itself, but excavation has revealed a foundation of squared blocks supporting a low sill of limestone blocks with the marks of a stone fence on the upper surface which formed the altar enclosure. Nearby is a statue base with a inscription that identifies the structure as the Altar of the Twelve Gods: "Leagros the son of Glaukon dedicated this to the Twelve Gods."

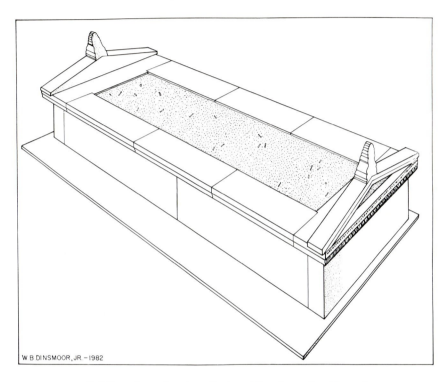

W.B. DINSMOOR, JR. – 1982

*3.5 Drawing of an inscribed molding from the Altar of Apollo Pythios. Drawing by William B. Dinsmoor, Jr.*

Literary sources tell us that the Altar of Apollo Pythios, like the Altar of the Twelve Gods, was built when Peisistratos the Younger was archon, in 522/1 B.C. Inscribed bases from the shrine survive and have been found near the Olympieion, so it is assumed that the altar was in that area. The inscription on the section of molding from the altar illustrated here reads: "This memorial of his office Peisistratos son of Hippias set up in the precinct of Pythian Apollo."

52

# 4

## OVERTHROW AND REVOLUTION

In 514 B.C. the tyrant Hipparchos was stabbed to death. The murder, actually the result of a love-feud, was quickly deemed a political act of assassination and the perpetrators, Harmodios and Aristogeiton, were proclaimed heroes and tyrannicides. Several years after the deed they were honored with statues set up in the middle of the Agora; Roman copies survive, as do representations painted on pottery (4.2, 4.3). Of the original bronze statues nothing remains but a small marble fragment of the inscribed base bearing the name of Harmodios and part of the honorary epigram (4.1).

The reign of the remaining tyrant, Hippias, became increasingly severe, as Aristotle records:

After this it began to come about that the tyranny was much harsher; for Hippias' numerous executions and sentences of exile in revenge for his brother led to his being suspicious of everybody and embittered. (*Athenian Constitution* 19.1)

One of the leading families in exile, the Alkmaeonidai, made several attempts to dislodge the tyrants. Herodotus regards them as more significant than the tyrannicides in bringing an end to the Peisistratid tyranny:

Indeed, in my judgement it was the Alkmaeonidai much more than Harmodios and Aristogeiton who liberated Athens; for the latter two by their murder of Hipparchos merely exasperated the remaining members of the clan, without in any way checking their despotism, while the Alkmaeonidai did, in plain fact, actually bring about the liberation. (*History of Greece* 6.123)

The liberation did not come easily. It took four years and several unsuccessful military encounters before the Alkmaeonidai, changing tactics, managed to bribe Apollo's oracle at Delphi to persuade the Spartans to help them oust the tyrants. For several decades the Spartans had enjoyed a reputation as the best warriors in Greece, and with the help of a Spartan army led by King Kleomenes the tyrants were thrown out in 510 B.C. Almost immediately, factional strife among the large families broke out once again, pitting the Alkmaeonid leader Kleisthenes against a certain Isagoras. At first Isagoras had the upper hand, until Kleisthenes enlisted the support of the common people by proposing a new constitution. Isagoras then called in the Spartans again. Kleomenes expelled 700 Athenian families, who joined Kleisthenes in exile. When Kleomenes and Isagoras tried to rescind the new Kleisthenic constitution, however, the Athenian people rose up in arms against them, threw the Spartans out, and recalled Kleisthenes.

But the Council resisted, and the multitude banded together, so the forces of Kleomenes and Isagoras took refuge in the Acropolis, and the people invested it and laid siege to it for two days. On the third day they let Kleomenes and his comrades go away under a truce, and sent for Kleisthenes and the other exiles to come back. The people having taken control of affairs, Kleisthenes was their leader and was head of the People. (*Athenian Constitution* 20.3.4)

These events, which took place between 508 and 507 B.C., culminated in the democratic form of government that we celebrate today.

The new democracy was called upon to defend itself immediately. King Kleomenes, angered at the outcome, returned with a large army in 507/6 B.C., allied with the Boiotians and the Chalkidians. A three-pronged attack was planned, but at the last minute objections by the Corinthians and the other Spartan king, Demaratos, led to the withdrawal of the Spartans. The Athenians fought and defeated both the Boiotians and Chalkidians on a single day. The credit for this great success was attributed by Herodotus to the new democracy:

Thus Athens went from strength to strength and proved, if proof were needed, how noble a thing freedom is, not in one respect only, but in all; for while they were oppressed under a despotic government, they had no better success in war than any of their neighbors, yet once the yoke was flung off, they proved the finest fighters in the world. (*History of Greece* 5.78)

*4.1 Fragment of an inscription from a statue base, about 475 B.C. L.: 0.323 m. Athens, Agora Museum I 3872.*

This fragment is probably part of the original base under the statues of Harmodios and Aristogeiton, who assassinated Hipparchos. Only part of the inscription is preserved, the name of Harmodios and the phrase "established their native land." A handbook of the Roman period on poetic meters, surviving in Renaissance copies, preserves more of the inscription:

A great light shone upon the Athenians when Aristogeiton and Harmodios slew Hipparchos.

Shortly after the assassination, the Athenians set up a pair of bronze statues of the Tyrannicides in the center of the Agora. This is one of the earliest known instances of honorary statues of mortals being set up in Athens, and it shows how significant the overthrow was to the young democracy. When the Persians sacked Athens in 480 B.C., they carried off the original statues to their capital at Susa. The Athenians soon replaced the group with another pair of statues, also of bronze. Later, after Alexander the Great's conquests in the East, the original group was returned to Athens, and both groups stood together in the Agora. Marble copies and fragmentary plaster casts of the Roman period reproduce one of the two groups (4.2). The importance of the monument to the democracy is attested by its appearance on vase paintings of the 5th and 4th centuries B.C. (4.3).

4.2 *Photograph of the Tyrannicides. Roman marble copy of a Greek bronze original of 490 or 475 B.C. H.: 1.85 m. (without base). Naples, Museo Archeologico Nazionale 44825.*

*4.3 Fragment of an Athenian (Attic) red-figure oinochoe
(jug), about 400 B.C. H.: 0.14 m. H.L. Pierce Fund.
Courtesy of the Museum of Fine Arts, Boston 98.936.*

The Tyrannicides are seen in profile in poses similar
to those of the figures in the Naples copy (4.2). The
lead figure, Harmodios, raises his right arm ready to
slash with a sword. Aristogeiton follows, sword held
low at his waist ready to thrust, his cloak over his
outstretched left arm. The figures are pictured on
a long, low base. Images of the Tyrannicides appear
on other vases of the late 5th century B.C., including
Panathenaic amphorae, the official prizes in the Panathenaic games. This vase is said to have been found
in the grave plot of an Athenian hero, Dexileos, who
died fighting at Corinth in 394 B.C.

*4.9 Photograph of a marble statue of a Spartan warrior, about 475 B.C. H: 0.78 m. Sparta Archaeological Museum.*

*4.4 Iron spearhead. L.: 0.215 m. Athens, Agora Museum IL 1057.*

*4.5 Bronze spear butt. L.: 0.216 m. Athens, Agora Museum B 1373.*

*4.6-8 Three bronze arrowheads. L.: 0.018-0.026 m. Athens, Agora Museum B 401, 438, 452.*

This marble sculpture, found on the acropolis of Sparta, is thought to represent a Spartan warrior. He wears a crested helmet and chest armor (*cuirass*); his eyes were once inlaid, perhaps with ivory or glass, to give a lifelike expression to the face. Spartan warriors helped overthrow the tyrants at Athens but were in turn expelled from Athens in the revolution.

# THE KLEISTHENIC REFORMS: CREATION OF THE DEMOCRACY

## CASES 5 AND 6

# 5

## THE TEN NEW TRIBES

Kleisthenes instituted a crucial reform, the reorganization of the citizenry into new administrative units called *phylai* (tribes). In his attempt to break up the aristocratic power structure, Kleisthenes abolished the use of the old Ionian tribes and created in their stead ten new ones. All citizens were assigned to one of these tribes, which were made up of members from each of the three geographical—and traditionally rival—areas of Attica: plain, coast, and hills. Political rights and many privileges depended on membership in one of the new tribes. Citizenship in Athens required prior enrollment in one of the tribes, and such membership was hereditary. A man served in the *Boule* (Senate) as a member of a tribe, and fought in the army—where his life literally depended in part on the shield of the next man in line—in a tribal contingent. Competitions in theatrical and athletic events were also carried out in tribal units. Privileges included access to common grazing land reserved for members of a tribe, as well as access to sacrifices and feasts held in honor of tribal heroes. Fighting, feasting, competing, and enjoying the advantages of citizenship together forged new bonds of loyalty to fellow tribesmen, even though they were from different regions of Attica and belonged to different clans. Old allegiances to the local aristocratic families were correspondingly weakened, and the new tribal system should be seen as an essential feature of the Athenian democracy.

Having created the ten tribes, Kleisthenes then sent to Apollo's oracle at Delphi the names of one hundred early Athenian heroes, and the oracle chose ten, after whom the tribes were named (5.2). Hence the term eponymous, which means giving one's name to something. The Eponymous Heroes were Hippothoon, Antiochos, Aias, Leos, Erechtheus, Aigeus, Oineus, Akamas, Kekrops, and Pandion (5.1). By the late 5th century a long base had been set up in the Agora to display statues of all ten heroes (5.3). This monument was one of the few allowed to stand within the limits of the open square, near the seat of government. The base became a public notice board: announcements concerning members of the tribes were hung on its front beneath the appropriate tribal hero. Thus, a member of the tribe of Leontis would find relevant notices beneath the statue of Leos: lists for military conscription, public honors, upcoming court appearances, and the like. More general announcements were also posted; in particular, legislation to be submitted to the *Ekklesia* (Assembly) was displayed at the Monument of the Eponymous Heroes for several days before the meeting so that citizens would have an opportunity to consider and discuss the proposals before voting. The base served as the prime source of official information within the city. Set in its prominent location, the Monument of the Eponymous Heroes was a crucial element in the dissemination of public information to the citizens of Athens and served also as the physical expression of the tribal system.

5.2 *Athenian (Attic) red-figure kylix (drinking cup), about 450 B.C., attributed to the Kodros Painter. H.: 0.125 m. Berlin, Antikenmuseum 2538.*

The picture shows a consultation with the oracle of Apollo at Delphi illustrating the way in which Kleisthenes might have received the names of the ten new tribes. The oracular priestess is seated on a tripod with high ring handles (the tripod is associated with Apollo). Her veiled head is bowed, and she holds a *phiale* (libation bowl) and a branch from Apollo's sacred tree, the laurel. On the right stands Aigeus, mythical king of Athens and father of the hero Theseus, about to receive the answer to his question.

*5.1 Athenian (Attic) red-figure kylix (drinking cup), about 480 B.C., signed by Douris as painter. H.: .133 m. Malibu, J. Paul Getty Museum 84.AE.569.*

On one of the exterior scenes of this drinking cup, two bearded figures are given the names of two of the eponymous heroes for whom two of the ten new tribes were named: Pandion and Kekrops, legendary kings of Athens and eponymous tribal heroes. The third male whose name is not inscribed may perhaps be understood as Erechtheus, another of the early kings of Athens. The central part of the picture shows the winged goddess of dawn, Eos, chasing the youth Kephalos, a scene of pursuit popular with vase painters although not usually represented with the accompanying male figures shown on this vase. Perhaps the vase painter added the figures with their names in order to make reference to the early kings and their connection with the ten tribes.

*5.3 Model of the Monument of the Eponymous Heroes in a 4th-century B.C. reconstruction. Model by Petros Demetriades and Kostas Papoulias. Athens, Agora Museum.*

The earliest references to a monument of the Eponymous Heroes came from the comic poet Aristophanes in the 420's B.C., but the foundations of the monument that have been excavated belong to the years around 330 B.C., nearly a century later. Located immediately east of the Metroon, the monument consisted of a base over 16 meters long that supported bronze statues of the ten heroes, with tripods at either end, presumably to reflect the role of Apollo's oracle at Delphi in their selection. The base was surrounded by a barrier of stone fence posts with wooden railings. All that is preserved today is the sill of the surrounding fence, several posts of marble and limestone, and several blocks from the base.

# 6

## POLITICAL ORGANIZATION OF ATTICA: DEMES AND TRIBAL REPRESENTATION

Each tribe was divided into three parts, and each third (*trittys*) was from one of the three regions of Attica, plain, coast, or hills. Every trittys was itself made up of several smaller units called *demes*. These were the old townships, villages, or neighborhoods which had existed for centuries. They were somewhat independent units with their own local officials and administrators (6.3-5), like any small town in the United States today. Altogether, there were about 140 demes in Attica, distributed among the ten new tribes. In some cases, when traditional ties between demes were particularly close, as, for instance, between Marathon and Probalinthos on the east coast of Attica, the new system usually had them assigned to separate tribes in an attempt to break such alliances. Surviving lists of tribesmen serving in the Boule (Senate) show that large demes regularly sent several representatives to serve each year, while small demes sent fewer, just as the number of congressmen and congresswomen from each state in our House of Representatives is determined by the population of the state. Acharnai in northern Attica was the largest deme, with twenty-two representatives (4% of the citizens of Attica), whereas many small demes sent a single representative or even alternated with another small deme.

This attempt to ensure equal representation is found throughout Athenian administration. Each jury in the lawcourts had an equal number of jurors from each of the ten tribes (see Case 9). Public offices were also apportioned out as fairly as possible. A good example of this concern with fairness is the fragmentary inscription (6.2) which records the transfer of the official weights and measures from the outgoing board of officials (*metronomoi*) to the incoming board. The five members and two secretaries of the metronomi are listed by name, patronymic (father's name), and deme and indicate that the seven came from seven different tribes:

The metronomoi when Archelaos was Archon:
Demostratos from Hestiaia
Aristokrates from Angele
Apollodoros son of Apollonios from
    Lamptrai
Theodotos from Ekale
Eratymenes from Oinoe
and the allotted secretary:
Nikias son of Philo from Kydathenaion
and the elected secretary:
Herakleitos son Timotheos from Krio
gave over the following weights and measures...

6.2 *Upper part of an inscribed marble stele (stone slab)
with red-painted letters, 222/1 B.C. H.: 0.275 m.
Athens, Agora Museum I 7030.*

Found inside the remains of the South Stoa, this inscription is a record of the metronomoi, the inspectors
of weights and measures, of whom Aristotle wrote in
the *Athenian Constitution* (51.2): "There are ten
metronomoi appointed by lot, five for the city and five
for Piraeus. They are responsible for all measures and
weights, to ensure that the salesmen use honest standards" (see Case 18.1-6).

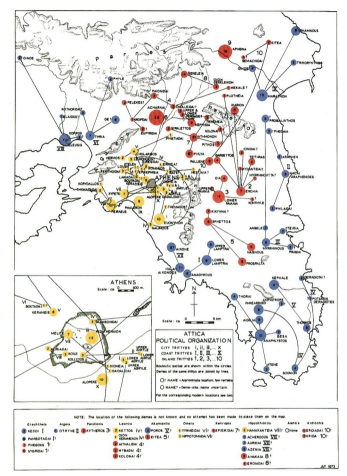

*6.1 Map of the Attic demes (neighborhoods). Drawn by John S. Traill,* Demos and Trittys, *Toronto, 1986.*

The map depicts Kleisthenes' new tribal system. Each color stands for a tribe. Each symbol represents an individual deme. The lines link the demes that make up each *trittys*. The mix of colors shows the broad geographical distribution of the three trittyses that make up each tribe. The number within each symbol indicates the number of senators sent annually from that deme to the Boule.

6.3-5 *Allotment tokens, 450-425 B.C. H.: 0.03 m. Athens, Agora Museum MC 820-822.*

These rectangular clay plaques cut with one jagged edge were probably used in connection with allotment of a deme office. On one side of each plaque the name of a tribe is written: ∟ΕΟ for the tribe of Leontis (6.3,4) and ΕΡΕ for the tribe of Erechtheis (6.5). On the other side is the name of the deme office: ΠΟ∟, probably *poletes*, an official auctioneer. ΗΑ∟ΙΜΟΣ is the name of a deme. The tokens were cut before firing in the kiln and would have been reunited in the process of allotting the deme office.

# 7

## THE EKKLESIA (CITIZENS' ASSEMBLY)

All Athenian citizens had the right to attend and vote in the *Ekklesia*, a full popular assembly which met about every 10 days. All decrees (*psephismata*) were ratified by the Ekklesia before becoming law.

As a rule, the Ekklesia met at its own special meeting place known as the *Pnyx*, a large theater-shaped area set into the long ridge west of the Acropolis (7.1). In theory every assembly represented the collective will of all the male citizens of Athens, although the actual capacity of the Pnyx never seems to have exceeded 13,500, and for much of the Classical period it held only about 6,000.

Throughout its long history the Pnyx had three major building phases (7.2). The earliest is generally associated with the Kleisthenic reforms. The second phase is dated to about 404/3 B.C., a time after the Peloponnesian War, when the democracy was abolished and Athens was under the control of the Thirty Tyrants, installed by Sparta. According to Plutarch, the Thirty had a specific political reason for shifting the orientation of the seating:

The Thirty afterwards turned the *bema* [stand for speakers] in the Pnyx, which was made to look at the sea, toward the land, because they thought that naval supremacy had been the origin of democracy but that tillers of the soil were less ill disposed toward oligarchy (*Life of Themistokles* 4).

The excavators associated this passage with a large stepped retaining wall designed to support a seating area that no longer followed the natural slope and that had the bema to the south, facing inland. In a third and final phase dated to the late 4th century B.C., the seating capacity was greatly increased, to accommodate as many as 13,500 people.

In an important democratic innovation, pay for attending the Ekklesia was instituted in about 400 B.C., thereby ensuring that everyone, including citizens of the working classes, could afford to participate in the political life of the city. Bronze or lead tokens (7.3-8) were issued to those attending the meeting, and these could later be redeemed for the assemblyman's pay of two obols (one-third of a drachma) per session.

*7.3-9 Lead tokens, 4th century B.C. D.: 0.015-0.023 m.*
*Athens, Agora Museum IL 656, 819, 893, 944,*
*1146, 1173, 1233.*

Decorated with various images—a bow, a cow, a dolphin, crossed torches, rosette, Nike, a ship, as well as letters (Ε or Κ)—these small tokens were turned in for pay, allowing poor citizens to participate without losing a day's wages.

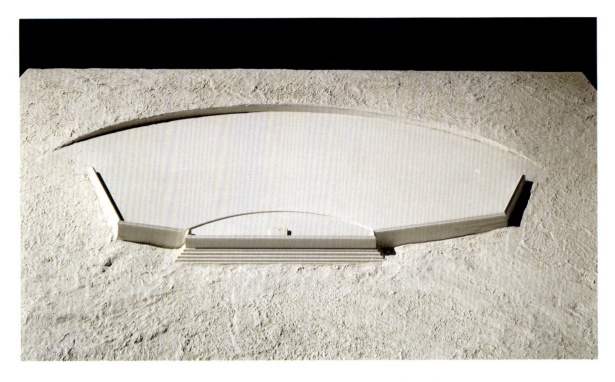

*7.1 The Pnyx, about 500 B.C. Model by C. Mammelis. Athens, Agora Museum.*

The model shows the Pnyx in its first phase, generally associated with the Kleisthenic reforms. The natural hill slope was used to form an auditorium, and there was a retaining wall at the bottom which supported the terrace where speakers stood. In this early form the seating capacity was about 5,000.

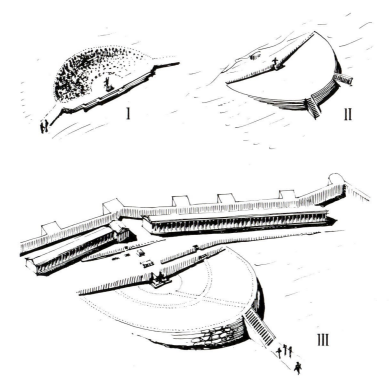

7.2 *Three phases of the Pnyx. Drawing by John Travlos.*

In phase I (about 500 B.C.) the Pnyx utilized the natural slope of the hillside, but either political concerns or the exposure of the seating area to northeast winds made a reversal of the structure necessary. In phase II (about 404/3 B.C.) an embankment with a retaining wall at the bottom created an auditorium with a slope contrary to that of the natural hillside, so that the audience now faced southwest and was sheltered from the winds. In phase III (4th century B.C.) the structure was enlarged but retained the same general configuration. Two large stoas were begun but never finished on the south side of the Pnyx adjacent to the city wall. Visible today are the foundation of the curved retaining wall of the auditorium of phase III and the rock-cut bema (stand for speakers), which projects from the scarp.

# 8

## THE BOULE (SENATE)

The Athenian legislature also included a deliberative body known as the Boule. It was made up of 500 members—50 from each of the 10 tribes—who were chosen by lot and served for the period of one year. The Boule would meet every day except festival days and propose legislation which was then ratified by all the citizens in the Ekklesia.

The Boule met in a building known as the *Bouleuterion*, which lay along the west side of the Agora square (8.2). It originally dated to the years around 500 B.C. and had simple wooden seating sufficient to accommodate the 500 members. During the first century of its use, it served also as a display area for numerous important documents, laws, and treaties:

> Nevertheless I still wish you to hear the words on the stone in the Bouleuterion concerning traitors and those who attempt to overthrow the democracy. . . . These words, gentlemen, they inscribed on the stone, and this stone they set up in the Bouleuterion (Lykourgos, [*Speech*] *Against Leokrates* 124, 126).

In the late 5th century a new Bouleuterion, immediately adjacent to the old one, was built to house the 500 senators. The Old Bouleuterion was then given over entirely to archival storage.

A fragmentary marble basin or perirrhanterion, marked as belonging to the Bouleuterion, presumably held the holy water in which the Athenians were accustomed to wash or dip their hands before entering any sacred space (8.1). Like most Athenian public buildings, the Bouleuterion was under the protection of the gods.

The deities of the Boule were Zeus Boulaios, Athena Boulaia, and Hestia (goddess of the hearth) Boulaia. Despite the religious aspects of the building, violence and sacrilege occurred occasionally during troubled political times, as in 404/3 B.C.:

> Theramenes leaped to Hestia Boulaia. . . [and] he was torn from the altars by those who had been so instructed and dragged through the middle of the Agora to his death (Diodoros Siculos 14.4.7, 5.3).

The Boule had a wide range of concerns and duties, such as overseeing the performance of magistrates, ensuring a sufficient food supply, and defending the country, including maintaining the fleet. Elections and much of the financial administration were also under the control of the Boule.

*8.1 Fragment of a marble basin, about 500 B.C. L.: 0.235
m. Athens, Agora Museum I 4869.*

The fragment preserves part of an inscription around
the rim which reads: OBOⱢEɎ, "of the Bouleuterion",
indicating ownership of the basin by the Senate, or
Boule. It was found just south of the foundations of
the Old Bouleuterion.

*8.2 The Old Bouleuterion, about 500 B.C. Model by Petros Demetriades and Kostas Papoulias. Athens, Agora Museum.*

Excavations have revealed the foundations of a nearly square building (23.30 m. X 23.80 m.), with a cross wall dividing the structure into a main chamber and entrance vestibule. The main room probably had five supports, although the foundations for only three have been found. There is no trace of seats, but they might be restored as rectilinear tiers of wooden benches on three sides.

8.3 *Reconstruction drawing of a meeting ·in· the Bouleuterion. Drawing by Richard Anderson. Agora Museum Archives.*

# 9

## THE PRYTANEIS
## (EXECUTIVE COMMITTEE OF THE SENATE)

The senators administered their meetings themselves. Each tribal contingent in the Boule served in rotation for a period of 35 or 36 days as the *Prytaneis,* or Executive Committee. During their time in office, the Prytaneis were responsible for day-to-day administration, the schedule, order of business and the like. The Prytaneis had their headquarters in the *Tholos,* a large round building which lay just adjacent to the Bouleuterion (9.1). During their term of office they were fed at public expense, and the Tholos served also as their dining hall. The meals were probably fairly modest in the beginning: cheese, barley cakes, olives, leeks, and wine, although by the late 5th century the menu also included fish and meat. Some of the tableware used at these public meals has been recovered from the vicinity of the building (9.2,3). The simple black-glaze cups, bowls, and pitchers have a ligature scratched or painted on them: ⅃ for *demosion* (public property), presumably so that the senators would not inadvertently walk off with the official crockery.

It is clear from written sources that the Tholos was used as a dining hall, but it is difficult to find a suitable arrangement for its furniture. Greeks usually ate reclining on couches (9.4), but there is no good arrangement whereby fifty couches can be made to fit into the building. It may be that in this instance the senators ate sitting up, on a bench around the inner face of the wall.

In addition to dining in the Tholos, at least one-third of the Prytaneis were expected to be on duty in the building at all times, so at least seventeen senators actually slept there at night. Thus, if some emergency arose either within the city or as a result of news from abroad, there were senators available at all times, ready to deal with it. The Tholos therefore in a sense represents the heart of the Athenian democracy, where common citizens were always on duty.

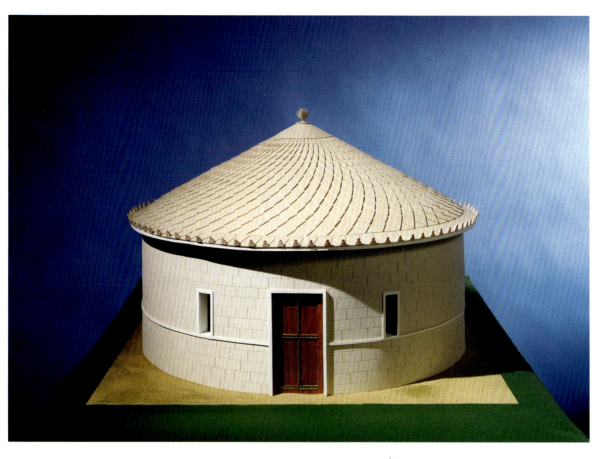

9.1 *The Tholos, about 470-460 B.C. Model by Petros Demetriades and Kostas Papoulias. Athens, Agora Museum.*

The circular shape of the Tholos is unusual among public buildings in the Agora. The design and construction are simple: the round chamber with an inner radius of 8.45 meters had a doorway on the east and six interior supports. The floor was clay. The building was famous for its roof shaped like a sun hat, which gave it the nickname *skias*, sunshade. The roof was made of diamond-shaped tiles, but their original arrangement is not known.

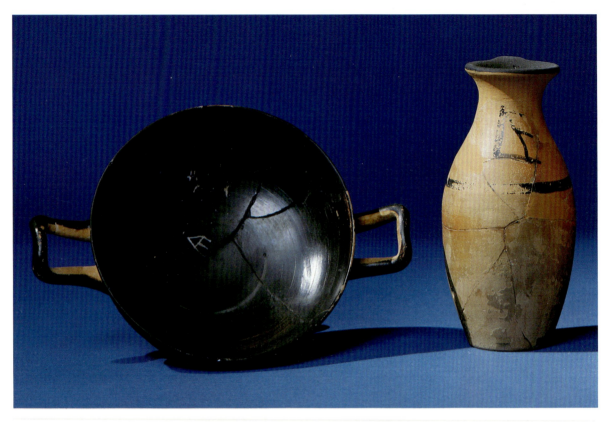

*9.2,3 Tholos dining ware, about 470-460 B.C.*

*9.2 Black-glaze kylix (drinking cup). H.: 0.077 m. Athens, Agora Museum P 5117.*

*9.3 Small olpe (jug). H.: 0.133m. Athens, Agora Museum P 13429.*

Both vases are marked with the ligature ⚹ for *demosion* (public property). On the black-glaze cup the inscription is incised with a sharp tool through the glaze, while on the jug the letters are painted in glaze. Both vases hold standard measures of liquid, suggesting their connection with the public kitchen and indicating that the democratic principle of a fair share for each was carried out.

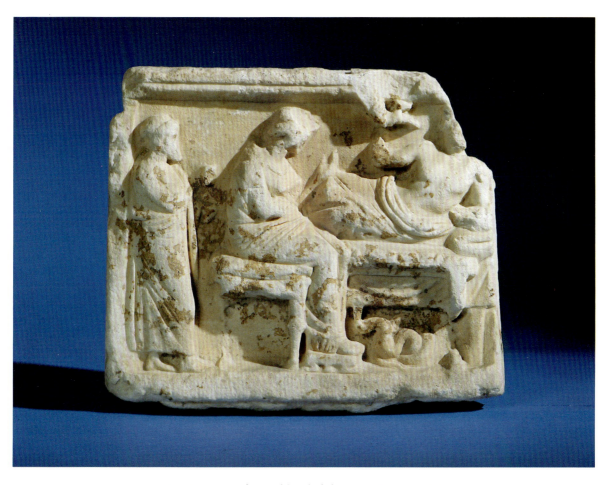

*9.4 Fragment of a marble relief showing a banquet, 4th century B.C. H.: 0.286 m. Athens, Agora Museum S 834.*

On the right, a man reclines on a couch behind a table. A woman sits on a stool nearby, with another male figure on the left. The senators must have eaten sitting upright, the pose in which women usually ate, since the size and circular plan of the Tholos would have made it difficult to accommodate the requisite number of couches.

# ATHENIAN DEMOCRACY: JUDICIARY
## CASES 10-13

# 10

## THE POPULAR COURTS

The popular courts, with juries of no fewer than 201 jurors and as many as 2,500, heard a variety of cases. The courts also had an important constitutional role in wielding ultimate authority by their interpretation of the laws, decrees, and decisions passed by the Ekklesia, Boule, and archons. It was not unlike the Supreme Court of the United States, which also examines individual cases of law and decisions passed by its Congress and approved by its President. Referring to the poorest citizens, Plutarch explains the significance of their participation in the courts from the time of Solon on as follows:

> All the rest were called Thetes; they were not allowed to hold any office but took part in the administration only as members of the Assembly and as jurors. This last privilege seemed at first of no account, but afterwards proved to be of the very highest importance, since most disputes finally came into the hands of these jurors. For even in cases which Solon assigned to the magistrates for decision, he allowed also an appeal to a popular court when anyone desired it. Besides, it is said that his laws were obscurely and ambiguously worded on purpose, to enhance the power of the popular courts. For since parties to a controversy could not get satisfaction from the laws, the result was that they always wanted jurors to decide it, and every dispute was laid before them, so that they were in a manner masters of the laws. (*Life of Solon* 18.2)

The lawcourts of Athens were scattered all over the city, but few have actually been excavated. Some certainly lay near the Agora and the association is ridiculed by the 4th century B.C. comic poet Euboulos:

You will find everything sold together in the same place at Athens—figs, summoners, bunches of grapes, pears, apples, witnesses, roses, loquats, haggis, honeycombs, chickpeas, lawsuits, milk, myrtle, allotment machines, hyacinth, lambs, waterclocks, laws, indictments. (Athenaeus, *Deipnosophistai* 14.640 b-c)

The court buildings themselves seem to have been large colonnaded structures where the hundreds of jurors could be accommodated on wooden benches. One such building has been found at the northeast corner of the Agora square (10.1). Other public buildings are also known to have been used for court sessions.

The courts were busy places as the Athenians, not unlike present-day citizens of the United States, were an extraordinarily litigious people:

They handle more public and private lawsuits and judicial investigations than the whole of the rest of mankind ("Xenophon," *Constitution of the Athenians* 3.2).

Court cases followed strict procedural rules. Before reaching a jury, the case was heard by a magistrate or arbitrators in a preliminary hearing. In some cases, the evidence presented, such as testimony of witnesses, was then sealed for presentation during the trial itself. The single lid of an unglazed cooking pot, although modest in appearance, seems to have been used in this sort of official capacity (10.2).

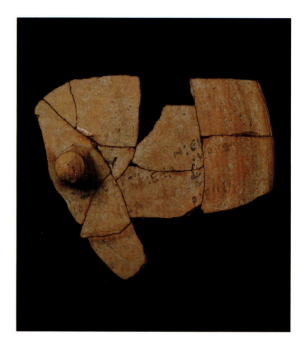

*10.2 Fragment from the inscribed lid of a cooking pot (echinus), 4th century B.C. L. of fragment: 0.113 m. Athens, Agora Museum P 28470.*

The inscription painted on the lid of this cooking pot seems to list documents that were stored in the pot until needed for a trial. The text reads: "Of the written copies, the following four are inside: *diamartyria* (testimony) from the *anakrisis* (arbitration), law on the abuse of heiresses, challenge of testimony, oaths of litigants; Antenor put the lid on." Names of litigants and, possibly, other relevant persons follow. We can infer that the evidence in this pot was used not only at public arbitration but at the trial as well.

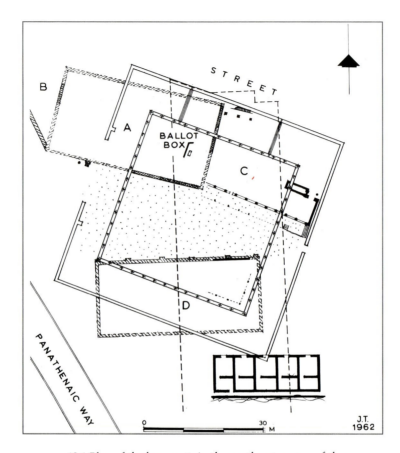

*10.1 Plan of the lawcourts in the northeast corner of the Agora. Drawing by John Travlos.*

Bronze ballots (13.1,2) and a ballot box (13.3) were found in a complex of rooms constructed in the late 5th and 4th centuries B.C. and identified on the basis of these finds as lawcourts. This original complex was replaced toward the end of the 4th century with a large colonnaded court, square in plan (38.75 m. on each side), each interior wall lined with columns. Individual courts may have functioned simultaneously in the various colonnades; the space between the columns and back wall on each of the four sides could have accommodated a court of 500 jurors.

*10.3 Pot. Athens, Agora Museum P 14655.*

Evidence for a trial may have been stored in pots of this
type.

# 11

# THE JURY

The jurors for each trial were chosen from a large body of citizens available for jury duty for the period of one year. At the beginning of the year, each juror was given a bronze *pinakion*, a plaque that had his name, father's name, and deme (and therefore tribe) inscribed on it (11.1). The pinakia were used in *kleroteria*, allotment machines that assigned jurors to the courts (11.2,3). The procedure worked as follows: On the day a trial was to be held, the potential juror would appear before the magistrate in charge of the allotment who was stationed at one of these machines. At the base of the kleroterion were ten baskets, one for each of the ten tribes. The pinakion would go into the appropriate tribal basket, which was labeled with the name of the juror's tribe. When it was time to allot jurors to courts, the magistrate would take the pinakia from the first tribal basket and put them into the first vertical row of slots in the machine, the pinakia from the second basket into the second row, and so on until he had placed all the pinakia into slots. Along the side of the machine was a hollow bronze tube, with a funnel at the top and a crank at the bottom. Into the funnel the magistrate poured a mixture of white and black marbles, which would line up in the tube in random order. A turn of the crank at the bottom produced a single ball. If it was white, the ten citizens (one from each tribe) whose pinakia were set into the first horizontal row would be assigned to the jury for that day and would proceed at once to the court. If it was a black ball, all citizens whose pinakia were in that row were dismissed for the day. The procedure was repeated until a court was filled, selecting ten jurors with every white ball.

The machine assured absolutely random selection, both in the order in which the pinakia were placed in the kleroterion and in the order in which the balls appeared. There was no easy way to bribe an Athenian jury, made up of at least 201 men chosen immediately before the court sat. At the same time, the kleroterion chose one juror from each of the ten tribes with each white ball, so that there was equal tribal representation on every court. The machine could also be used to appoint a board of ten magistrates, in this case only one of the balls would be white. As much as any object left to us from antiquity, the kleroterion indicates the lengths to which the Athenians went in trying both to ensure equality and to forestall corruption in their governmental affairs.

Athenian jurors were paid, another democratic procedure designed to ensure that all could afford to serve. Small round lead tokens or *symbola* were issued to jurors who had been allotted to assure proper payment to the right individuals (11.4-6). Payment was made only at the end of the trial and only upon presentation of the symbolon. Numerous symbola have been found scattered over the Agora; they carry different devices and letters to indicate the court to which the juror was assigned.

*11.1 Bronze juror's ticket (pinakion), 4th century B.C. L.:
0.102 m. Athens, Agora Museum B 822.*

This identification ticket carries the juror's name:
Demophanes; the first letters of his father's name:
Phil....; and his deme: Kephisia.

*11.4-6 Lead lawcourt tokens, 4th century B.C. D.: 0.016-
0.017 m. Athens, Agora Museum IL 587, 716, 941.*

According to Aristotle, the juror on entering the court
received a token, or symbolon (*Athenian Constitution*
65, 68, 69). After voting he turned in the token and was
thus entitled to receive his fee of three obols (one-half
a drachma). Some fifty such tokens have come to light
in the Agora, most dating to the 4th and early 3rd century B.C. On those illustrated here a letter appears on
one side, a kappa: K, or an epsilon: E, indicating the
court to which the juror was assigned or a particular
seating area within the court.

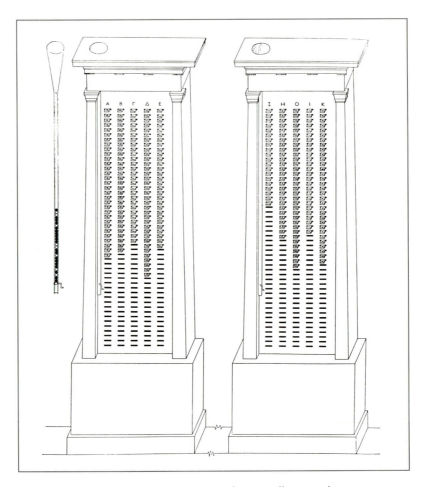

*11.2 Reconstruction drawing of a jury-allotment device (kleroterion). Agora Museum Archives.*

Ten rows of narrow slots were used to hold the juror's tickets. The hollow tube held black and white balls. When cranked, a black or white ball issued forth, determining who would serve that day. The machine assured random selection of the jury and equal tribal representation. According to Aristotle, a pair of such kleroteria stood at the entrance to each court (*Athenian Constitution* 63).

*11.3 Fragment of a jury-allotment device (kleroterion), about 200 B.C. H.: 0.38 m. Athens, Epigraphical Museum 13255.*

This marble fragment preserves two rows of slots and a tube for the black and white marbles used in the selection procedure. With only two rather than ten rows of slots, this kleroterion was probably used for choosing magistrates or tribes rather than in the selection of a jury. At least seventeen fragments of kleroteria have been found in Athens, fourteen in the Agora. Most of the surviving examples date to the 2nd century B.C., although their existence is documented earlier by Aristotle (*Athenian Constitution* 63, 64, 66). The earlier examples were movable and probably were made of wood, which would help explain why they have not survived.

# 12

## THE SPEAKERS

Litigants spoke on their own behalf, although occasionally using speeches prepared by trained professionals; skillful rhetoric was necessary in order to sway a jury. The speeches written by several noted orators survive today, those of Lysias, Lykourgos, Hypereides, Antiphon, Demosthenes, Aeschines, and Isokrates. Of these, perhaps the best known for his ability in forensic speaking was Demosthenes, a statesman who led Athenian opposition to the rising power of Philip of Macedon in the 4th century B.C. (12.4).

Demosthenes' skills as a public speaker in the assembly were honed by training and considerable self-discipline:

> They say that when he was still a young man he withdrew into a cave and studied there, shaving half of his head to keep himself from going out; also that he slept on a narrow bed in order to get up quickly and that since he could not pronounce the sound of R he learned to do so by hard work, and since in declaiming for practice he made an awkward movement with his shoulder, he put an end to the habit by fastening a split or, as some say, a dagger from the ceiling to make him through fear keep his shoulder motionless. They say, too, that as he progressed in his ability to speak he had a mirror made as large as himself and kept his eyes on it while practicing, that

he might correct his faults; and that he used to go down to the shore at Phaleron and address his remarks to the roar of the waves, that he might not be disconcerted if the people should ever make a disturbance; and that because he was short of breath he paid Neoptolemos the actor ten thousand drachmas to teach him to speak whole paragraphs without taking breath. (Plutarch, *Moralia* 844)

No trial took more than a single day. Time was therefore allotted to the speakers according to a set schedule and measured carefully by means of *klepsydrai* (waterclocks): "There are klepsydrai that have small tubes for the overflow; into these they pour the water by which the lawsuits must be conducted" (Aristotle, *Athenian Constitution* 67.2). A single example has survived, dating to about 400 B.C. (12.1,2). It runs for only six minutes and thus represents a short speech. The preserved speeches of Demosthenes and other orators, whether on public or private matters, run much longer, and there must have been larger vessels to time them. Testimony of witnesses and citation of legal documents did not count against one's speaking time, and there are repeated requests in the preserved speeches for the water to be stopped. Experienced orators would keep an eye on the jet of water at the outlet, and as the pressure fell they would bring their speech to an end just as the last drops ran out.

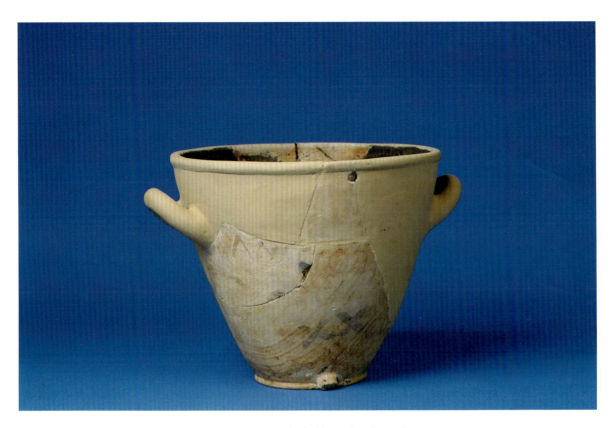

*12.1 Fragmentary waterclock (klepsydra), late 5th century B.C. H.: 0.172 m. Athens, Agora Museum P 2084.*

The clay fragment preserves the base and part of the wall of a deep bowl. It is identified as part of a waterclock by the clay spout fitted with a small bronze inner tube just above the base. Centered above the spout, just below the rim, is a hole that would permit the pot to be filled to the same level each time. The pot bears two inscriptions. Near the bottom, *X X*, the letter chi, which must stand for *Χous* (choes), which was a measure of about 3.2 liters. Since the pot held two choes, its total capacity was about 6.4 liters, which takes about six minutes to run out. The other inscription, *A N T I O . . .* indicates that the waterclock belonged to the tribe Antiochis.

*12.2 Photograph of a reconstructed waterclock in action. Athens, Agora excavations.*

This replica shows how the waterclock worked. The pot at the higher level would be filled with water, and the speaker spoke until all the water had run into the pot at the lower level.

*12.4 Gold ring with a carnelian stone, late 1st century B.C. D.: 0.034 m. Collection of the J. Paul Getty Museum, Malibu 90.AN.13.*

Demosthenes was one of a select number of Greek poets, philosophers, and public figures to appear on Roman gemstones. Among the others were the philosophers Sokrates, Aristotle, Epikouros, and the playwright Menander. The signature of the engraver, Apelles, an otherwise unknown gem engraver of the Roman period, appears under the shoulder of Demosthenes. Apelles adapted this portrait in profile from the famous 3rd-century B.C. statue by Polyeuktos (12.3).

12.3 *Photograph of a statue of Demosthenes. H. including plinth: 2.2 m. Copenhagen, Ny Carlsberg Glyptothek IN 2780.*

The statue is a Roman copy that probably goes back to a Greek original attributed to the sculptor Polyeuktos, erected in the Agora in 280 B.C. The face is that of a man 50 to 60 years of age with lean, lined cheeks and short, curly hair and beard. His eyes are deep-set and placed close together, with crow's feet at the outer corners. His forehead is furrowed, and his thin lips are partly covered by a mustache. His expression suggests the determination of his character as described in ancient sources. Demosthenes was one of the great orators of all time and is best remembered for his political speeches in which he urged the Athenians to live up to their democratic ideals of equality and liberty. He was also an advocate in private court cases on such subjects as inheritance, fraud, forgery, and assault. At least fifty marble portraits of Demosthenes survive; most have been found in Italy, attesting to his great popularity in Roman times.

# 13

## THE VERDICT

After the speeches and other evidence had been presented, the members of the jury voted by casting ballots. A series of vase paintings of the early 5th century B.C. show a mythological story, the vote for the arms of Achilles. In these scenes the Greek heroes vote using pebbles, observed by many bystanders (13.4), suggesting that the concept of a secret ballot did not yet exist. Whether or not the voting scenes that appear on vases depicting this story show an actual method of voting in early 5th-century Athens, their appearance at this time may have been prompted by the enhanced importance of voting that resulted from the reforms of Kleisthenes.

The voting scene in Aeschylos' play *Eumenides*, produced in 458 B.C., suggests that by this time a means of voting secretly existed. We are told that in voting on whether Orestes should live or die, the contesting parties placed their ballots (pebbles or mussel shells) into one of two urns, one for the prosecutor, the other for the defendant. Although it is hard to see how this procedure could be secret, since the choice of urn might be observed by anyone present, it seems that the Athenians had devised a way to maintain secrecy, for in the vote over Orestes' fate, the outcome is in doubt until the votes are counted. Athena, casting her vote in Orestes' favor, says:

> If the other votes are even, then Orestes wins.
> You of the jurymen who have this duty assigned,
> Shake out the ballots from the vessels, with all speed.
> (Aeschylos, *Eumenides* 740-743, translated by Richard Lattimore)

By the mid-4th century B.C. the system had changed to that described by Aristotle:

> There are bronze ballots, with an axle through the middle, half of them hollow

and half solid. When the speeches have been made, the men appointed by lot to take charge of the ballots give each juror two ballots, one hollow and one solid, in full view of the litigants so that no one shall take two solid or two hollow. . . . There are two jars in the court, one of bronze and one of wood. . . . The jurors cast their votes in these: the bronze jar counts and wooden does not; the bronze one has a pierced attachment through which only one ballot can pass, so that one man cannot cast two votes. When the jurors are ready to vote, the herald first makes a proclamation, to ask whether the litigants object to the testimonies: objections are not allowed once the voting has begun. Then he makes another proclamation: 'The hollow ballot is for the litigant who spoke first (prosecutor), the solid for the one who spoke afterwards (defendant).' The juror takes his ballots together from the stand, gripping the axle of the ballot and not showing the contestants which is the hollow and which is the solid, and drops the one that is to count into the bronze jar and the one that is not into the wooden. (*Athenian Constitution* 68, translated by P.J. Rhodes)

If the vote was for guilty, then there was a second phase of the trial to set the penalty. After additional speeches, the jury then decided between two punishments, one proposed by the prosecution, the other by the defense. If the prosecutor failed to get a sufficient number of guilty votes— at least one fifth—his case was deemed unworthy, and he himself was fined.

Some forty-eight ballots fitting Aristotle's description have been found in the Agora, some actually inscribed "official ballot" (13.1,2). A ballot box has also been identified (13.3).

*13.3 Photograph of a ballot box. L.: .70 m. Athens, Agora excavations.*

This container, in which six bronze ballots were found including those described above (13.1,2), is made of two terracotta drain tiles set on end.

*13.1,2 Bronze ballots, 4th century B.C. D.: 0.06 m. Athens, Agora Museum B 728, 1056.*

One ballot has a solid axle, the other a hollow axle. The ballot with the solid axle bears the letter epsilon, E, which might designate a jury section, or, more likely, a tribe. The ballot with the pierced axle is inscribed: "psephos demosia," public ballot. Most of the ballots uncovered in the Agora are of bronze, but a few are of lead. The majority are datable to the 4th century B.C., but the latest, and especially those of lead, may run into the 2nd century B.C.

*13.4 Photograph of Athenian (Attic) red-figure kylix (drinking cup), signed by Douris as painter, about 490 B.C. H.: 0.12 m. Vienna, Kunsthistorisches Museum 3695.*

The picture on one side of the exterior shows the Greek heroes voting to decide who should receive the armor of Achilles, greatest of the Greek heroes to fight at Troy. Athena presides over the voting stand in the center. Two heroes vote, each adding a pebble to a different pile. Other heroes wait their turn, one already holding his ballot. The contestants appear at either end of the picture: Odysseus, the winner, raises his hands in glee, while Ajax, the loser, bows his head in sorrow.

Achilles' armor was supposed to go to the Greek warrior most feared by the Trojans. According to the extant literary sources, the decision was to have been reached either by overhearing a conversation between two Trojan girls, one of whom was inspired by Athena to praise Odysseus above Ajax, or by asking a group of Trojan prisoners whom they feared the most. In suggesting that the decision was made by a pebble vote, the vase painter may be reflecting the increased importance of voting in the new democracy. Douris and the other vase painters of the first decade of the 5th century B.C. who depict this scene are using a mythological story to comment on contemporary events.

# THE PROTECTION OF DEMOCRACY

## CASES 14–17

# 14

## OSTRACISM

Soon after their victory over the Persians at the battle of Marathon in 490 B.C., the Athenians began the practice of ostracism, a form of election designed to curb the power of any rising tyrant. They were probably inspired at least in part by the fact that their old tyrant Hippias, who had been thrown out years before, accompanied the Persian fleet to Marathon, hoping to be reinstalled in power in Athens once again.

The procedure of ostracism was simple. Once a year the people would meet in the Agora and take a vote to determine if anyone was becoming too powerful and was in a position to establish a tyranny. If a simple majority voted yes, they met again in the Agora two months later. At this second meeting each citizen carried with him an

*ostrakon* (potsherd) on which he had scratched the name of the person he wished ostracized. If at least 6,000 votes were cast, the man with the most votes lost and was exiled for ten years. The procedure was used frequently in the 480's and less often thereafter. While an interesting idea, it did not really work to curb ambition in the long run, for a prominent man, if powerful enough, could use it to eliminate his chief rival. Such an occurrence is recorded in 443 B.C., when Perikles was facing vociferous criticism of his policies, especially his building program. An ostracism was held, which resulted in the exile of his main opponent, Thucydides the son of Melesias (not Thucydides the historian). Plutarch describes the final ostracism and the abandonment of the procedure in 417 B.C.:

Now the sentence of ostracism was not a chastisement of base practices, instead it was speciously called a humbling and docking of oppressive prestige and power; but it was really a merciful exorcism of the spirit of jealous hate, which thus vented its malignant desire to injure, not in some irreparable evil, but in a mere change of residence for ten years. And when ignoble men of the baser sort came to be subjected to this penalty, it ceased to be inflicted at all, and Hyperbolos was the last to be thus ostracized. It is said that Hyperbolos was ostracized for the following reason. Alkibiades and Nikias had the greatest power in the state and were at odds. Accordingly, when the people were about to exercise the ostracism, and were clearly going to vote against one or the other of these two men, they came to terms with one another, united their opposing factions, and effected the ostracism of Hyperbolos. The people were incensed at this for they felt that the institution had been insulted and abused, and so they abandoned it utterly and put an end to it. (*Life of Aristeides* 7.3-4)

Useless immediately after the counting, the actual *ostraka* were simply discarded in the street or any convenient hole. Like most baked pottery, ostraka are virtually indestructable; excavations in Athens have produced over 11,000 examples. More than any literary text, the ostraka bring to life a sense of Athenian power politics as waged centuries ago. They preserve the names of all the well-known statesmen as well as several unknown aspirants to political power (14.1-10).

*14.1 Ostrakon of Megakles, ostracized in 486 B.C. Max. dim.: 0.11 m. Athens, Agora Museum P 14490.*

Inscribed ΜΕΓΑΚΛΕƧ ΗΙΓΓΟΚΡΑΤΕƧ, Megakles son of Hippokrates. Aristotle reports the ostracism of Megakles son of Hippokrates, and goes on to say that "the Athenians continued for three years to ostracize the friends of the tyrants, on account of whom the law had been enacted" (*Athenian Constitution* 22). More than 4,000 ostraka bearing Megakles' name were found in one deposit in the Kerameikos (the potters' quarter of Athens) and have been associated with the ostracism of 486 B.C., although the rude comments that accompany his name on some of these ostraka concentrate on his morals rather than on his tyrannical tendencies.

*14.3 Ostrakon of Xanthippos, ostracized in 484 B.C. Max. dim.: 0.073 m. Athens, Agora Museum P 6107.*

Inscribed: ΧƧΑΝΘΙΓΓΟƧ ΑΡΡΙΦΡΟΝΟƧ, Xanthippos son of Arriphron. Aristotle says that after three years of concentrating on ostracizing the friends of the tyrants, the Athenians "took to removing anyone else who seemed too powerful: the first man unconnected with the tyranny to be ostracized was Xanthippos son of Arriphron" (*Athenian Constitution* 22).

*14.4 Ostrakon of Aristeides, ostracized in 482 B.C. Max. dim.: 0.125 m. Athens, Agora Museum P 9973.*

Inscribed: ΑΡΙΣΤΕΙΔΕΣ ΛVΣΙΜΑ+Ο, Aristeides son of Lysimachos. Plutarch tells an anecdote about the ostracism of Aristeides:

> . . . while the votes were being written down, an illiterate and uncouth rustic handed his piece of earthenware to Aristeides and asked him to write the name Aristeides on it. The latter was astonished and asked the man what harm Aristeides had ever done him. "None whatever," was the reply, "I do not even know the fellow, but I am sick of hearing him called 'The Just' everywhere." When he heard this, Aristeides said nothing, but wrote his name on the ostrakon and handed it back. (*Aristeides* 7, translated by Ian Scott-Kilvert)

*14.5 Ostrakon of Kimon, ostracized in 461 B.C. Max. dim.: 0.106 m. Athens, Agora Museum P 18555.*

Inscribed : ΚΙΜΟΝ ΜΙΑΤΙΑΔΟ, Kimon son of Miltiades. Kimon, influential statesman and soldier of the 470's and 460's B.C., was the leader of an aristocratic faction, which brought him into opposition with Perikles and other democrats and eventually led to his ostracism. He was recalled before five years had elapsed.

*14.2 Ostrakon of Hippokrates, candidate for ostracism in the 480's B.C. Max. dim.: 0.10 m. Athens, Agora Museum P 6036.*

Inscribed twice ΗΙΠΠΟΚΡΑΤΕΣ ΑΛΚΜΕΟΝΙΔΟ, Hippokrates son of Alkmeonides. This Hippokrates is not otherwise known, but he must have been a member of the Alkmeonid family and, like the father of Megakles (14.1), may have had a connection to the Peisistratid tyrants.

14.6 *Ostrakon of Perikles, candidate for ostracism in the mid-5th century B.C. Max. dim.: 0.07 m. Athens, Agora Museum P 16755.*

Inscribed: ΓΕΡΙΚΛΕΣ +ΖΑΝΘΙΓΓΟ, Perikles son of Xanthippos. After Kimon's ostracism, Perikles rose to power as leader of the democratic party. Elected *strategos* (general) year after year, he diverted the funds of the Delian League, established for the defense of Greece, to magnificent building programs in Athens, among them the rebuilding of the Acropolis. He may often have been a candidate for ostracism but was never ostracized.

14.7 *Ostrakon of Thucydides, ostracized in 443 B.C. Max. dim.: 0.13 m. Athens, Agora Museum P 29461.*

Inscribed: ΘΟΚΥΔΙΔΗΣ, Thucydides. This Thucydides, the son of Melesias, may have been the maternal grandfather of the historian Thucydides. He was opposed to Perikles and especially to his building program. His ostracism left Perikles as the uncontested political leader of the Athenian state.

*14.9 Ostrakon of Alkibiades, candidate for ostracism in 417-415 B.C. Max. dim.: 0.074 m. Athens, Agora Museum P 29373.*

Inscribed: ΑΛΚΙΒΙΑΔΗΣ ΚΛΕΙΝΙΟ, Alkibiades son of Kleinias. Although he avoided ostracism, Alkibiades did not retain the trust of the Athenians. The historian Thucydides says that:

> The masses, afraid of the greatness of his lawless and sensual self-indulgence in this manner of living . . . became hostile to him on the grounds that he was aiming at a tyranny; and though publicly he managed the affairs of war most excellently, in his private life every man had been offended at his practices (*History of the Peloponnesian War* 6.15.3-4, translated by Charles Forster Smith).

*14.8 Ostrakon of Nikias, candidate for ostracism in 417-415 B.C. Max. dim.: 0.085 m. Athens, Agora Museum P 31179.*

Inscribed: ΝΙΚΙΑΙ ΝΙΚΗΡΑΤΟ, Nikias son of Nikeratos. Nikias, politician and general during the Peloponnesian War, concluded a peace settlement with Sparta known as the Peace of Nikias in 421 B.C. Sometime between 417 and 415 he allied himself with Alkibiades in order to avoid ostracism and later sailed with him on the ill-fated Sicilian expedition, only to lose the war and his life at the hands of the Syracusans in 413 B.C. According to some, this was due to his inadequacy as a military leader.

*14.10 Athenian (Attic) red-figure kylix (drinking cup), about 470 B.C., attributed to the Pan Painter. D.: 0.26 m. Oxford, Ashmolean Museum 1911.617.*

A man holding a stylus and a writing tablet stands behind a low table on which rests a *krater* (mixing bowl) containing small, irregular red objects. More of the same objects are lying on the table, and a boy is approaching with a shallow bowl containing another batch of them. To the left are two other figures, the first holding more of the red objects, the second, an elderly, bald man, taking down a writing case. This unique scene has been identified as the counting of votes at an ostracism. The man with the stylus and writing tablet would be tallying the votes. This identification of the subject has not found universal acceptance. Others have suggested that is represents a cult scene or a sacrifice at an unidentified festival.

# 15

## FACTIONAL POLITICS:
## THE OSTRACISM OF THEMISTOKLES

A group of ostraka found together in a pit on the North Slope of the Acropolis is of special interest. There were 190 ostraka, mostly the round feet of drinking cups, all inscribed with the name of Themistokles son of Neokles, of the deme Phrearrhios, the far-sighted architect of Athenian naval power. The picture of party politics comes into sharper focus when one carefully examines the handwriting, for these 190 ostraka were written by only fourteen people. Three samples from each of four hands are represented in the 12 ostraka here; letter forms and sizes as well as incised lines show the characteristics of individual handwriting. The deposit apparently represents the leftovers of a plot to remove Themistokles; his enemies were equipped in advance with ready-made ostraka for distribution to illiterate or undecided voters.

The democratic voters of Classical Athens were as fickle as electorates elsewhere at other times. Though never ostracized, even Perikles was voted out of office after winning fifteen consecutive annual elections. Seen in retrospect, Themistokles was as great a figure in Athenian history. When a great find of silver was made in southern Attica, it was he who convinced the Athenians not to distribute the money among themselves but to spend it building a great fleet of 200 *triremes* (war-

ships). These ships proved crucial in the decisive victory of the Greek fleet over the Persians at Salamis in 480 B.C., as did Themistokles' own guile in tricking the Persians into fighting in the narrow straits.

> But that the salvation which the Hellenes achieved at that time came from the sea, and that it was those very triremes that restored again the fallen city of Athens, Xerxes himself bore witness, not to speak of other proofs. (Plutarch, *Life of Themistokles* 4.4)

Despite his extraordinary success in turning Athens into the dominant sea power, which led to her military success throughout the 5th century, Themistokles made numerous personal enemies, and we hear disparaging remarks about his greed and ambition. Finally, he was ostracized in 472 B.C. and died in exile several years later, fulfilling the prophecy of his father as preserved in the following anecdote:

> There are some who say that his father fondly tried to divert him from public life, pointing out to him old triremes on the seashore, all wrecked and neglected, and intimating that the people treated their leaders in like fashion when these were past service (Plutarch, *Life of Themistokles* 2.6).

*15.14 Photograph of a marble bust of Themistokles. H.: 0.50 m. Italy, Ostia Museum. Courtesy of the German Archaeological Institute, Rome.*

The bust, inscribed at the bottom with the name of Themistokles, is a Roman copy of a Greek original of about 470-460 B.C. The original was probably made while Themistokles was still living and is remarkable for that period in its realistic representation, which shows something of the man's character. Thucydides says that Themistokles was "both a shrewd judge of the immediate present, and wise in forecasting what would happen in the most distant future" (*History of the Peloponnesian War* 1.138.3, translated by C.F. Smith).

15.1 *Ostrakon of Themistokles, candidate for ostracism in the 480's, ostracized in 472 B.C. Max. dim.: 0.10 m. Athens, Agora Museum P 9950.*

Inscribed: ΘΕΜΙSΘΟΚLΕΕS ΝΕΟΚLΕΟS ΦΡΕΡΙΟS, Themistokles son of Neokles of Phrearrhios. The large number of ostraka bearing Themistokles' name found in the Agora and elsewhere (a total of 2,279) indicate that he was often a candidate for ostracism, especially in the 480's when his hawkish policies met with opposition.

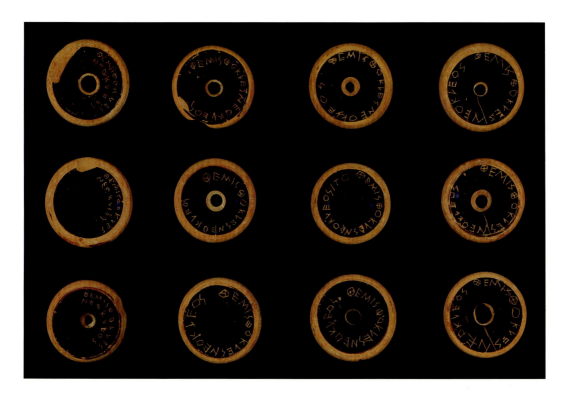

*15.2-13 Ostraka of Themistokles*

A group of 190 ostraka bearing the name of Themistokles were found in a well on the North Slope of the Acropolis. The similarity of these 190 ostraka to one another suggests that they are not merely a chance collection but were made as a group that for one reason or another was never used but was disposed of in the well. The ostraka demonstrate remarkable uniformity in the form and content of the inscriptions. Fourteen different "hands" can be distinguished, showing that the ostraka were prepared by a relatively small number of people, whether to distribute at an ostracism or for some other purpose. Three ostraka by each of four different hands are represented here.

*Hand A: Three kylix bases, D.: 0.062-0.075 m. Athens, Agora Museum AO 12, 13, 16.*

Note the theta, mostly circular but occasionally square, cross-barred, with upright or St. Andrew's cross.

*Hand B: Three kylix bases, D.: 0.062-0.075 m. Athens, Agora Museum AO 21, 49, 91.*

The letters of Hand B are similar but slightly smaller than those of Hand A.

*Hand C: Three kylix bases, D.: 0.062-0.075 m. Athens, Agora Museum AO 3, 64, 121.*

In this hand the theta is circular, made with a single stroke leaving an opening at top or bottom, with a Y-shaped cross bar.

*Hand E: Three kylix bases, D.: 0.062-0.075 m. Athens, Agora Museum AO 11, 33, 82.*

The letters are small and written with a very fine point.

# 16

## THE ATHENIAN ARMY

From the very beginning, the Athenians were compelled to fight for their new democracy (Case 4); their dramatic victories over the Boiotians and Chalkidians in 506 B.C. led many to attribute Athenian military success to their political system. This notion was greatly enhanced by the extraordinary victory of the Athenian army over the Persians at Marathon in 490 B.C. On numerous subsequent occasions, Athenian citizens were called upon to go into battle against other states, both Greek and foreign, most often against oligarchies and aristocracies, since the Athenians tended to ally themselves with other democracies.

The army was managed by the polemarch, together with ten generals, one elected from each of the tribes. In their attempt to ensure equality, the Athenians by the 5th century allotted most offices, even the highest archonships. Some positions, however, such as treasurers and the water commissioner, were simply too important to be left to the luck of the draw; these remained elective and therefore became real positions of power whereby a politician demonstrated popular support and remained in office for many years. The generalships are the clearest example of this practice, and many of the leading statesmen of Athens held the position. Perikles, for instance, never served as eponymous archon—nominally the highest post in the state—but he was elected general of his tribe year after year, and from that position he guided Athenian affairs for decades. By far the largest component of the army was the infantry composed of *hoplites*, citizens fighting in a full set of armor. They went into battle protected by a helmet, breastplate, and greaves (shin guards), carrying a large round shield and long thrusting spear (16.20,21). On occasion, the state would issue such equipment to citizens who could not afford a set of their own (16.12-18).

Citizens received military training during their service as *ephebes* from age 18 to 20:

The people elect two athletic trainers and in-
structors for them, to teach them their drill
as heavy-armed soldiers and to use the bow,
javelin, and sling. . . . They go on in this
mode of life for the first year; in the following year an assembly is held in the theater,
and the ephebes give a display of drill before
the people and receive a shield and spear
from the state and they then serve on patrols
in the country and are quartered at the
guard-posts. Their service on patrol goes on
for two years; the uniform is a mantle; they
are exempt from all taxes. . . . When the
two years are up, they now are members of
the general body of citizens. (Aristotle, *Athenian Constitution* 42.2-5)

Richer Athenians enrolled in the cavalry, as
always, a smaller elite military force made up of
those wealthy enough to own and maintain a
good mount (16.19 and 2.2). The state carried out
an inspection and registered each horse on an annual basis, so that the owner could draw a
maintenance allowance. Several dozen lead strips
recording the color, brand, and value of the
cavalry mounts have been found in the Agora,
where the cavalry trained (16.1). Here, too, were
found the clay disks stamped with the name of
the *hipparch* (cavalry commander) Pheidon
(16.4-11). The 4th-century B.C. historian Xenophon
describes the duties of a cavalry commander:

First, he must sacrifice to propitiate the gods
on behalf of the cavalry; second, he must
make the processions during the festivals
worth seeing; further, he must conduct all
the other obligatory displays before the people with as much splendour as possible (*The
Cavalry Commander* 3.1, translated by E.C.
Marchand).

16.21 *Fragment of an Athenian (Attic) red-figure bell-
krater (mixing bowl), 5th century B.C. H.: 0.127 m.
Athens, Agora Museum P 15837.*

A warrior with helmet, sword in scabbard, spear and
shield (device: snake) attacks an opponent to the left
(now missing).

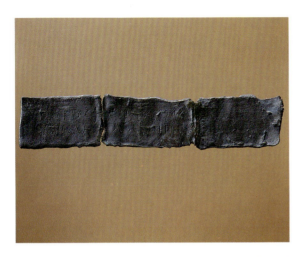

*16.1 Inscribed lead strip from the cavalry records, 4th century B.C. L.: 0.073 m. Athens, Agora Museum IL 1563.*

Recovered from a well in the northwest corner of the Agora, this lead strip carries an inscription recording the registration of a horse. On one side is the name of the owner, Konon; on the other a description of the horse, a chestnut, with a centaur brand, as well as its price, 700 drachmas. Such strips were clearly used for the annual assessment of the cavalry and would then form the basis of a reimbursement by the state should the horse be lost in battle. At the end of the year these records would become obsolete and could be reused or discarded, as in the case of this example found in a well. From the series of similar strips recovered in Athens we learn that the maximum assessment of a horse was 1,200 drachmas, well below the value of many horses and representing the maximum limit of the state's responsibility; the minimum amount was 500 drachmas.

*16.12-18 Lead armor tokens, 3rd century B.C. D.: 0.018-0.021 m. Athens, Agora Museum IL 1575 (helmet), 1573-1574 (breastplate), 1579 (shield), and 1572, 1576-1577 (greave).*

Each token is stamped on both sides. On one side a piece of armor is shown: a helmet, breastplate, shield, or greave, and on the other side, the letter A (alpha), Γ (gamma), or Δ (delta). These tokens might have been used as exchanges for state-owned armor. The letters may have designated sizes for the armor pictured on the other side. Public armor was most likely kept on hand for the arming of irregulars, thetes, and perhaps even slaves, at the time of mobilization, whereas Athenians on the official hoplite register were legally responsible for procuring their own military equipment. By the 3rd century B.C. there was only a small standing army, so the number of irregulars must have grown to include much of the city's middle-class population.

*16.2,3 Clay tokens or passports of a border commander, 4th century B.C. D.: 0.039-0.04 m. Athens, Agora Museum SS 8080, MC 1245.*

The tokens were inscribed with the name of Xenokles, his deme, Perithoidai, and his title, *Peripolarch*. The peripolarch was the military officer responsible for the frontier garrisons and the border patrols. These tokens were probably used as passports and for messengers reporting to and from military headquarters.

*16.4-11 Clay tokens of a cavalry commander, 4th century B.C. D.: 0.029-0.034 m. Athens, Agora Museum MC 1164-1165, 1169-1170, 1179, 1183, 1189, 1190.*

The tokens are stamped with the title, hipparch, cavalry commander; his assignment: "at Lemnos;" and the man's name and deme: Pheidon of Thria. The eight examples reproduced here are part of a group of thirty similar tokens found in the same well, at a level dating to the second half of the 4th century B.C., as the inscribed lead strip describing Konon's horse (16.1) During the 4th century, the cavalry commander at Lemnos was not only one of the principal officers of the cavalry but also the ranking Athenian official on the island. In a remarkable example of correlation between archaeological and literary evidence, Pheidon may be the same individual mentioned in a fragment of the 4th-century B.C. comic poet Mnesimachos, who wrote: "Go forth, Manes, to the Agora, to the Herms, the place frequented by the phylarchs (other cavalry commanders), and to their handsome pupils whom Pheidon trains in mounting and dismounting" (Athenaios, *Deipnosophistai* 9.402).

*16.19 Athenian (Attic) red-figure oinochoe (jug), late 5th century B.C. H.: 0.14 m. Athens, Agora Museum P 23850.*

The horse, led by a boy holding a victor's wreath, is probably the winner of a race or other equine event.

*16.20 Athenian (Attic) red-figure lekythos (oil container), late 6th century B.C., attributed to the Roundabout Painter. H.: 0.138 m. Athens, Agora Museum P 24061.*

The Roundabout Painter was named for this vase, which shows three warriors and a trumpeter running around the body of the jug. The warriors wear helmets and greaves, and carry shields ornamented with various devices: an anchor, insect, or serpent.

# 17

## THE ATHENIAN NAVY

With thousands of kilometers of coastline and hundreds of islands, the Greek world was likely to be dominated only by a naval power. A generation after the establishment of democracy Athens became such a power under the influence of Themistokles. The fleet was made up of triremes, wooden warships that carried 170 rowers manning three banks of oars. The ships were 100-120 feet long and about 20 feet wide. At her peak, Athens had a fleet of 400 ships, a force requiring close to 80,000 men. These rowers, mainly drawn from Athens' poorer citizens, were paid and were seldom slaves. These citizen oarsmen were recognized as early as the 5th century B.C. as a significant force in the maintenance of the democracy.

Now, in discussing the Athenian constitution, I cannot commend their present method of running the state, because in choosing it they preferred that the masses should do better than the respectable citizens; this, then, is my reason for not commending it. Since, however, they have made this choice, I will demonstrate how well they preserve their constitution and handle the other affairs for which the rest of the Greeks criticize them.

My first point is that it is right that the poor and the ordinary people there should have more power than the noble and the rich, because it is the ordinary people who man the fleet and bring the city her power; they provide the helmsmen, the boatswains, the junior officers, the look-outs and the shipwrights; it is these people who make the city powerful much more than the hoplites and the noble and respectable citizens. This being so, it seems just that all should share in public office by lot and by election, and that any citizen who wishes should be able to speak in the Assembly. ("Xenophon," *Constitution of the Athenians* 1.1-2)

Oared ships appear on Athenian vases from the 8th to the 5th century B.C. (17.2,3), and several of the 372 shipsheds that lined the harbors of the Piraeus have been excavated. These sources, supplemented with ancient descriptions and inscriptions listing naval equipment, allow an accurate reconstruction of one of these ancient warships (17.1).

*17.2 Two fragments (nearly joining) of an Athenian (Attic) Geometric krater, 8th century B.C. H. of left fragment 0.22 m. H. of right fragment: 0.15 m. L. both fragments together: 0.38 m. Athens, National Archaeological Museum 802.*

The two fragments show a warship with a ram sailing to the left. The sail, represented by hatched horizontal and vertical lines, is raised. The hull and ram of the ship are shown in profile, whereas the vertical and horizontal lines above the hull are thought to represent the ship in plan, as if seen from above; thus, the thick horizontal line represents the other side of the ship, and the vertical lines depict the benches where the rowers sat.

In the stern, at the right the helmsman holds the sail with one hand and the sailyard brace with the other. Part of the steering oars can be observed on the right edge of the fragment. The fragments come from the lower part of a large funerary krater decorated with several warships, which may allude to how the deceased, whose grave this krater marked, met his death.

*17.3 Fragment of an Athenian (Attic) red-figure votive shield, about 460 B.C. L.: 0.089 m. Athens, National Archaeological Museum 1072.*

The fragment, found on the Athenian Acropolis, shows a woman or perhaps the goddess Nike (Victory) holding in each hand an *aphlaston*, the upright ornament from the stern of a ship, here probably the spoils of Persian ships captured by the Athenian navy. The *aphlasta* are decorated with human faces.

*17.1 Model of a trireme. Model by Aristoteles and George Rallis.*

The trireme was the warship that brought Athens preeminence in Greek waters in the 5th and 4th centuries B.C. The ship was designed for speed, lightness, and ease of manoeuvre. With the three tiers of rowers that give the trireme its name, the ship acted as an oar-powered battering ram manned by highly trained and disciplined rowers.

*17.4 Photograph of a trireme under sail. Paul Lipke, The Trireme Trust.*

The reconstructed trireme shown in this photograph was built under the supervision of John Morrison, a classical scholar, and John Coates, a naval architect. It is now a vessel in the Greek Navy and is manned by international crews of rowers for sea trials each summer. The structure of the ship is based on a study both of the archaeological evidence and of the historical accounts of sea battles.

# 18

## ADMINISTRATION AND BUREAUCRACY

The economy of Athens was supervised by numerous boards of officials in charge of the mint, the marketplace, weights and measures, and the grain and water supplies. Most of these officials held office in or near the Agora, where so much of the city's commercial activity took place.

One function of the Tholos was to serve as a repository for official weights and measures under the supervision of the inspectors, the metronomoi (see Cases 6 and 9). According to ancient sources, sets of official weights and measures were kept in Athens as well as at Piraeus and Eleusis. Many small weights, mostly of lead but also of bronze, have been found in and around the Agora. Some may belong to the primary sets kept permanently in the Tholos (18.1-3), but many are probably duplicates made for issue to officials and perhaps shopkeepers. They have been found scattered over a wide area, as if they had been used in the market or shops.

Official measures come in clay and bronze and were used both for dry goods (nuts, grain) and for liquids (wine, oil) (18.4-6). Dry measures normally had a cylindrical or mug-like form; liquid measures, much less abundant, were in the shapes of jugs, amphoras, or other vessels (18.6). Clay measures were found concentrated around the Tholos.

Large deposits of silver from mines at Laureion in South Attica provided Athens with abundant coinage admired for its purity and used throughout the Mediterranean (18.7-15). The coin type was appropriate to Athens and easily recognizable: on one side the helmeted head of Athena, patroness of the city, on the other side her sacred symbols, the owl and olive sprig. These figures were used for centuries with only the slightest changes. The coins were struck in a wide variety of multiples or fractions of the basic unit, the drachma, which was roughly a day's wage. This silver coinage, which probably began in the 6th century B.C., continued to be minted for some 500 years.

*18.1-3 Set of official weights, about 500 B.C. Stater: 0.063 m. X 0.064 m.; quarter: 0.039 m. X 0.039 m.; sixth: 0.033 m. X 0.034 m. Athens, Agora Museum B 495, 492, 497.*

This set of official bronze weights, found near the Tholos, dates to the early years of the democracy. Each weight carries not only an inscription giving the name of the weight but also a symbol in high relief, which served both as a visual key to the particular unit or fraction and for the benefit of the illiterate. The stater has a knucklebone as symbol and weighs 795 grams. The quarter, with a shield, weighs 190 grams. The sixth, with the turtle, weighs 126 grams. The weights are close, but not exact, fractions of the stater. The weights are also inscribed with the phrase *demosion Athenaion,* "public (property) of the Athenians."

*18.4 Bronze public measure, about 400 B.C. H.: 0.09 m. Athens, Agora Museum B 1082.*

This example of a dry measure bears an inscription on the upper collar stating that it is the official measure of the Athenians. The cylindrical shape is well adapted both for emptying and leveling off. This example holds about 1/4 pint.

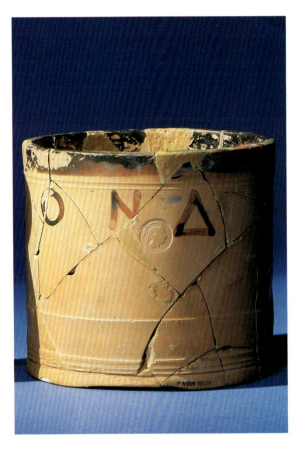

*18.5 Clay public measure, second half of the 4th century B.C. H.: 0.132 m. Athens, Agora Museum P 3559.*

The cylindrical dry measure is inscribed *demosion*, indicating that it is official. Validating stamps that guarantee the capacity of the measure appear between the letters of the inscription: the head of Athena and a double-bodied owl. The capacity of this measure is about 1 1/2 quarts.

*18.6 Photograph of a public measure. Munich, Staatliche Antikensammlungen 9406.*

Probably a liquid measure, this vase, an amphora, is decorated with the owl associated with Athena and inscribed *demosion*, indicating its official use.

*18.7-15 Silver and bronze coins of Athens, 5th-3rd centuries B.C. Athens, Agora Museum C 212, 214, 564, 232-237.*

The earliest coin in this group is a silver obol of the time of Solon (C 232) with an amphora on the obverse and an incuse square on the reverse. The other eight coins show the head of Athena, goddess and patroness of Athens, and the owl, her sacred bird:

C 236: silver obol, about 450 B.C., Athena and owl.
C 235: silver triobol, mid-5th century B.C., Athena and owl.

C 234: silver drachma, second half of 5th century B.C., Athena and owl.
C 233: silver tetradrachma, second half of 5th century B.C., Athena and owl.
C 237: silver tetradrachma, first half of 4th century B.C., Athena and owl.
C 212: bronze fraction, 3rd century B.C., Athena and owl.
C 214: bronze fraction, 3rd century B.C., Athena and double-bodied owl.
C 564: silver tetrobol, 3rd century B.C., two owls and Athena.

# 19

## STATE RELIGION: THE ARCHON BASILEUS

There was no attempt in Classical Athens to separate church and state. Altars and shrines were intermingled with the public areas and buildings of the city. A single magistrate, the archon Basileus or king archon, was responsible for both religious matters and the laws; appointed by lot, he served for a year. Aristotle describes his varied duties as follows:

> The basileus is first responsible for the Mysteries, in conjunction with the overseers elected by the people . . . also for the Dionysia at the Lenaion, which involves a procession and contest. . . . He also organizes all the torch races and one might say that he administers all the traditional sacrifices. Public lawsuits fall to him on charges of impiety and when a man is involved in a dispute with someone over a priesthood. He holds the adjudications for clans and for priests in all their disputes on religious matters. Also all private suits for homicide fall to him. (*Athenian Constitution* 57)

The king archon held office in the Royal Stoa, a small colonnaded building along the west side of the Agora square (19.2). It was built at about the same time as the Kleisthenic reforms, in about 500 B.C. In addition to housing the king archon, the stoa served also to display the laws of Athens. In the late 5th century B.C. the Athenians inscribed their constitution on stones and set them up inside and in front of the Royal Stoa so any Athenian could come and read the laws of the city.

In addition, several ancient texts refer to the great unworked stone (lithos) found in place in front of the building (19.3), which was used by the king archon when, as chief of the religious magistrates, he administered their oath of office: "They took the oath near the Royal Stoa, on the stone on which were the parts of the (sacrificial) victims, swearing that they would guard the laws" (Pollux 8.86) and "the Council took a joint oath to ratify the laws of Solon, and each of the thesmothetes swore separately at the stone in the Agora" (Plutarch, *Life of Solon* 25.2).

The stoa was the setting for events that led to the trial and death of Sokrates in 399 B.C. The philosopher was tried for impiety, for importing new gods into the city, and for corrupting the youth of Athens. These were religious matters and as such fell under the jurisdiction of the king archon. Preliminary arguments were held in the Royal Stoa, as we learn from Plato, quoting Sokrates: "Now I must present myself at the Stoa of the Basileus to answer the indictment which Meletos has brought against me" (*Theatetos* 201D)

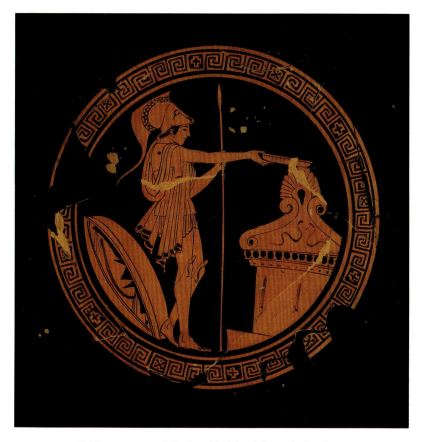

*19.1 Fragmentary Athenian (Attic) red-figure kylix (drinking cup), about 475 B.C. H.: 0.097 m. Athens, Agora Museum P 42.*

It was important for Athenian citizens, especially warriors departing for battle, to render the gods their due. Here, a young warrior offers a libation at an elaborate altar topped with scrolls and a palmette finial and smeared with the blood of previous sacrifices. The warrior holds a spear in one hand and a phiale (libation bowl) in the other. He wears a short tunic with a cloak over his shoulders, a helmet, and greaves. His shield, shown in a perspective, three-quarter view, is behind him.

*19.2 The Royal Stoa (Stoa Basileos) in the late 6th century B.C. Model by Petros Demetriades and Kostas Papoulias. Athens, Agora Museum.*

The earliest and simplest of the stoas that bordered the Agora, the Stoa Basileos had eight Doric columns between its two end walls; the stumps of the columns can still be seen. There were four inner columns evenly spaced within the length of the building; these, too, were Doric. Continuous benches ran along the back and across the ends of the building. The 2nd-century A.D. traveler Pausanias identified the stoa clearly: "The first (building) on the right is the stoa called Basileos, where sits the 'King' (Basileus) when he holds the annual magistery called 'Kingship' " (*Description of Greece* 1.3.1). Pausanias describes several clay akroterion figures on the roof of the stoa; fragments of these have been found. They represented the Athenian hero Theseus hurling the brigand Skiron into the sea, and Eos, goddess of dawn, carrying off Kephalos (compare 5.1).

*19.3 Photograph of the Lithos, or Oath Stone, late 6th century B.C. L.: 3.0 m. Athens, Agora excavations.*

Although its top is level and smooth, the stone is unworked, a condition appropriate to its sacred function. The stone lies in front of the Royal Stoa and is clearly the stone on which magistrates stood to take the oath of office.

*19.4 Reconstruction drawing of the northwest corner of the Agora, ca. 300 B.C. Drawing by W. B. Dinsmoor, Jr.*

The Royal Stoa is at the upper left. At the upper right is the Painted Stoa, birthplace of Stoic philosophy, and in the foreground is a crossroads shrine.

# CRITICISM OF DEMOCRACY

## CASES 20–23

# 20

## SOKRATES

The philosopher Sokrates was one of many Athenians critical of the people and their control over affairs of state. His probing public debates with fellow citizens led to his trial for impiety and corrupting the youth of Athens, his approach and opinions having exceeded the limits on freedom of speech acceptable to the Athenians. The Agora, as the political center of Athens, was the scene of many of the events played out in the drama of his teaching, trial, and death.

According to custom, youths were not expected to spend time in the great square; the gymnasia of the city—the Academy and Lyceum—were their proper haunts. Sokrates, therefore, met them in a shop near the Agora, according to Xenophon (*Memorabilia* 4.21), and Diogenes Laertios preserves the name of Simon as the owner of the establishment where these meetings took place: "Simon, an Athenian, a shoemaker. When Sokrates came to his workshop and discoursed, he used to make notes of what he remembered, whence these dialogues were called 'The Shoemakers'" (2.13.122). Regrettably, the shoemaker dialogues have not survived, but in the excavations of the Agora, a small house of the 5th century B.C. was excavated east of the Tholos, just outside the Agora boundary stone (20.2-5). Within it were found bone eyelets and iron hobnails clearly used for shoemaking, and nearby was found the broken fragment of a drinking cup, inscribed with the name of the owner, "Simon." The archaeological evidence suggests that we have here the very shop, visited by Perikles, which Sokrates used as an informal classroom, meeting here those students too young to frequent the square.

The preliminary indictment leading to Sokrates' trial took place in the Royal Stoa (Case 19), and he was tried before a jury of 501 Athenians, in one of the lawcourts of the city, not as yet excavated. The trial was fairly close: 221 to 280 votes, according to Sokrates; in the penalty phase of the trial, however, he was condemned to death. According to Athenian law, the defense could propose an alternate penalty (see Case 8). Plato, in the *Apology*, tells what Sokrates suggests:

> What penalty do I deserve to pay or suffer, in view of what I have done? . . . I tried to persuade each one of you not to think more of practical advantages than of his mental and moral well-being, or in general to think more of advantage than of well-being in the case of the state or of anything else. . . . What else is appropriate for a poor man who is a public benefactor and who requires leisure for giving you moral encouragement? Nothing could be more appropriate for such a person than free maintenance at the state's expense (*Apology* 36B, translated by Hugh Tredennick).

Sokrates' confinement and execution in the state prison of Athens are described in some detail by Plato, and his description corresponds in several respects to a large building lying southwest of the Agora square. Here were found the thirteen little clay medicine bottles that may have held the poison hemlock with which the Athenians dispatched their political prisoners (20.6-18), and here, too, was found the small marble statuette that closely resembles the known portraits of Sokrates (20.1).

*20.1 Photograph of a bust of Sokrates, Roman copy of a Greek original of the mid-4th century B.C. H.: 0.77 m. Naples, National Archaeological Museum 6415. Photograph courtesy of the German Archaeological Institute, Rome.*

This bust is thought to reflect a Greek bronze original of the mid-4th century B.C. by the sculptor Lysippos.

Sokrates, whose conversations and teachings were recorded by Plato and Xenophon, was said to have been bald, with a broad nose and wide, open nostrils, prominent eyeballs, a large mouth with thick lips, and a pot belly. Xenophon's *Symposion* gives the best evidence for Sokrates' appearance, in a dialogue where beauty is defined in functional terms: "Your eyes see only straight ahead, but mine see also to the side, since they project. . . . Your nostrils look to the ground, but mine flare so as to receive smells from all sides. . . . My flat nose does not block my vision but allows my eyes to see whatever they wish" (Xenophon, *Symposion* 5.5-7).

The Naples bust is inscribed with Sokrates' name and with a quotation from his speech in prison as recorded by Plato: "I am not for the first time but always a man who follows nothing but the reason which on consideration seems to be the best" (Plato, *Krito* 46B).

*20.2 Photograph of the House of Simon the Shoemaker. Athens, Agora excavations.*

The photograph shows the foundations of a house to the left of a roadway. It has been identified as a shoemaker's establishment by the discovery in the rooms of iron hobnails (20.4) and bone shoelace eyelets (20.5). The base of a black-glaze drinking cup found in the roadway is inscribed "of Simon" (20.3), so it seems likely that this was the house of Simon the Shoemaker to whom the literary texts refer.

20.3 Base of an Athenian (Attic) black-glaze kylix (drinking cup), 5th century B.C. D.: 0.073 m. Athens,
Agora Museum P 22998.

The inscription ΣΙΜΟΝΟΣ, "of Simon," is scratched
on the upper surface of the cup base. The cup can be
dated by details of its shape to about 460 B.C., a time
rather earlier than would be consistent with the Simon
known to Sokrates and mentioned in the literary
sources. It has been suggested that by the end of the
5th century, the base had become separated from the
bowl of the cup and had been reused as a door knocker.
The name Simon thus indicates whose house it was,
and the findspot in the roadway is logical.

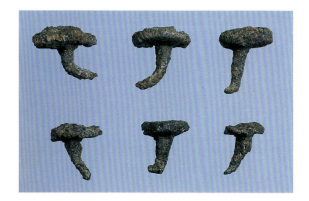

20.4 Iron hobnails, 5th century B.C. L. of shafts: 0.015
m. Athens, Agora Museum IL 1361.

20.5 Bone shoelace eyelets, 5th century B.C. D.:
0.015-0.025 m. Athens, Agora Museum BI 738.

*20.6-18 Set of thirteen clay medicine bottles, 4th century B.C. H.: 0.036-0.042 m. Athens, Agora Museum P 20858.*

These small bottles are of a type generally used for drugs and medicine. This set of thirteen, found in the annex to the state prison, may have been used to hold the hemlock that was measured out in the exact dose necessary to cause death. After his trial in 399 B.C., recorded in Plato's *Apology*, Sokrates was executed in this manner.

*20.19 Fragmentary marble statuette, 4th century B.C. H.: 0.105 m. Athens, Agora Museum S 1413.*

Only one statue of Sokrates is recorded in ancient literature. After executing him, the Athenians felt such remorse that eventually they commissioned a bronze statue of Sokrates, the work of the renowned sculptor Lysippos, which they set up in the Pompeion in Athens (Diogenes Laertios 2.43). A bust in Naples may reproduce the original by Lysippos (20.1). This small statuette found in the state prison may have been a memento recalling the Lysippan bronze.

# 21

## THEATER

Western drama was an Athenian invention which developed late in the 6th century B.C. out of the festivals celebrated in honor of the god Dionysos. Originally held in the Agora, the plays were soon transferred to the South Slope of the Acropolis, where a theater holding close to 15,000 people was constructed (21.8). In a characteristic attempt to ensure full participation by the citizens, those eligible were paid to attend the dramatic performances.

In addition to several dozen surviving tragedies by Aeschylos, Sophokles, and Euripides and comedies by Aristophanes and Menander, our knowledge of Athenian theater is enhanced by the dozens of small terracotta figurines and masks depicting the numerous stock characters who appeared in the plays (21.2-8). The large numbers of surviving examples indicate how important theater was in the life of an Athenian citizen. As today, it must have been a powerful force for the molding of public opinion, particularly since it was state-sponsored. Before large audiences comic poets such as Aristophanes filled their plays with stinging criticism of all the leading politicians of 5th-century Athens, as well as the assemblymen and jurors:

They encourage personal attacks if anyone wished, knowing that the butts of comedy are not for the most part of the common people nor from the masses, but rich or noble or powerful; only a few of the poor, ordinary citizens are attacked in comedy, and they only because they meddle in everything or try to become too influential; therefore the people do not object even to the ridiculing of such men. ("Xenophon," *Constitution of the Athenians* 2.18)

Many of the comedies satirizing democracy and its practitioners were awarded prizes for excellence in dramas such as Aristophanes' *Knights*, produced in 424 B.C.:

We have a master, boorish, angry, a bean-eater, irascible: Demos of the Pnyx, a difficult old man and rather deaf. (lines 40-43)

An inscribed base set up by the King Archon Onesippos on the steps of the Royal Stoa (19.2) records the results of the dramatic festivals he administered in his year in office (21.9). In the ancient counterpart of our Academy Awards, we can read the names of the winning producers and playwrights in both comedy and tragedy in a year around 400 B.C. The winning comic poet, Nikochares, was a contemporary and rival of Aristophanes.

*21.1-5 Terracotta statuettes and molds for statuettes of actors.*

Four of these terracottas date to the 4th century B.C. and can be associated with the so-called Middle Comedy represented by Aristophanes' last two plays, *Assemblywomen* (Ekklesiazusae) and *Wealth* (Ploutos), and the various fragments from plays that are not preserved in their entirety. The statuettes represented add new types to those known from the literary sources and enrich our picture of the Athenian theater during the 4th century.

*21.1 Statuette of a traveler, about 375 B.C. H.: 0.073 m. Athens, Agora Museum T 1685.*

This traveler or traveler's servant wears a traveling cap, tunic, and cloak, and he carries a flask and basket that hang in front of him. This was a popular figure in Old Comedy as well. We can imagine the overburdened servant complaining as Xanthias did in Aristophanes' *Frogs*: "I'm the ass they tie outside the gate. Damned if I tote this stuff another yard."

*21.2 Statuette of an old man, about 375 B.C. H.: 0.075 m. Athens, Agora Museum T 1683.*

Sporting a long beard and wearing tunic and cloak, this old man has his hand to his brow as if spying something: "Who by the entrance doth palely loiter?" (Aristophanes, *Wasps*).

*21.4 Statuette of a slave seated on an altar, about 330 B.C. H.: 0.055 m. Athens, Agora Museum T 1742.*

The legs and altar have been restored according to other versions of this type. This popular figure represents an impudent slave who has fled to the household altar where he can enjoy immunity from punishment. His hand is up to his ear, as if nursing it after it has been boxed.

*21.5 Statuette of Herakles, 300-250 B.C. H.: 0.08 m. Athens, Agora Museum T 862.*

This figure represents a tragic actor playing the role of Herakles. Traces of the lionskin the hero usually wears are visible at his hairline. His left hand is wrapped in his cloak, and his right arm is raised, perhaps once holding a club. An actor might have taken this stance to deliver the lines in Euripides' *Hercules Furens*: "But—for now the action of my hand is needed—I will first go and destroy the palace of the new king, cut off his unhallowed head, and throw it to the dogs to tear."

130

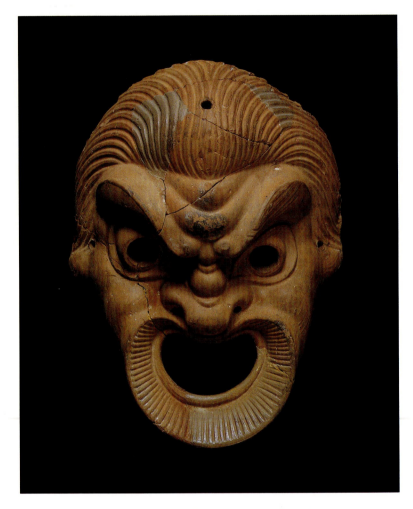

*21.6 Terracotta mask of the Leading Slave, about 250 B.C.
H.: 0.27 m. Athens, Agora Museum T 478.*

The mask is characterized by the slightly twisted,
trumpet-shaped mouth typical of slave masks. The hair
has been combed back from the forehead, and a short
beard frames the mouth. The mask is lifesize but was
probably not used as a mask but as a votive gift to be
hung on a wall.

*21.7 Fragmentary mold with a relief scene, A.D. 250-267.
L.: 0.08 m. Athens, Agora Museum T 2404.*

The mold shows a masked woman lying on a couch, a wreath in her right hand. A male figure wearing the mask of a slave sits at the foot of the couch. The Latin inscription, "Comedia Pylades," may refer to the names of the two actors represented. Pylades, whose name suggests his Greek origin, takes the part of a slave. Comedia may be the name of an actress. Women were unknown on the Greek stage, where female roles were always taken by male actors, but by the time this mold was made, there is evidence that women performed publicly and may well have acted on the stage. This mold might commemorate two actors in a Roman troupe who performed in Athens in the second half of the 3rd century of our era.

*21.8 Photograph of the Theater of Dionysos on the south
slope of the Acropolis. Photograph by Alison Frantz.*

The masterpieces of Aeschylos, Sophokles, Euripides,
and Aristophanes were first performed here. The
theater was rebuilt in the 4th century B.C. to replace
an earlier structure and was extensively modified in
Roman times.

*21.3 Mold for a statuette of a seated slave, about 350 B.C. H.: 0.067 m. Athens, Agora Museum T 2059.*

This fragmentary mold represents a slave seated with his legs crossed. He may be part of a set for a mythological comedy that parodied the story of Herakles and Auge.

*21.9 Photograph of a statue base set up to commemorate Onesippos' term as king archon, about 400 B.C. Athens, Agora excavations.*

Listed are the names of the winning producers and playwrights for both comedy and tragedy.

# 22

## THE UNENFRANCHISED, I - WOMEN

Numerous people resident in Athens and Attica had little part in the political life of the state. Most glaring by modern standards was the exclusion of women, although a similar exclusion persisted into the 20th century in Western society: Women only received the vote in all states of the United States in 1920, in France in 1945, and in Switzerland in 1971. Though protected by numerous laws regarding her property and rights, Athenian women had no vote and were not allowed to participate actively in political life. Women were not expected in the Agora, and it is not entirely clear that they were allowed to attend the theater. The proper Athenian lady was expected to spend almost all her time at home, and her primary function was to bear and raise the children. Perikles' comment on women in his great funeral oration is illuminating:

> If I am to speak also of womanly virtues, referring to those of you who will henceforth be in widowhood, I will sum up all in a brief admonition: Great is your glory if you fall not below the standard which nature has set for your sex, and great also is hers of whom there is least talk among men whether in praise or in blame. (*Thucydides* 2.45)

In addition to her duties as mother, the average Athenian woman was expected to run the household, an extraordinarily time-consuming operation. In addition to cleaning and preparing food, this meant making most of the family clothing on the loom and fetching drinking water from one of the local fountainhouses.

Only in the area of religion did women have a direct role in public life. They were active participants in most of the cults and their associated festivals. Several of the significant cults had priestesses rather than priests as the chief religious functionaries.

Needless to say, there were exceptions to the rule, and the famous women of Athens about whom anything was written were infamous, including—ironically—Perikles' own companion Aspasia:

> Sources claim that Aspasia was highly valued by Perikles because she was clever and politically astute. After all, Sokrates sometimes visited her, bringing along his pupils, and his close friends took their wives to listen to her—although she ran an establishment which was neither orderly nor respectable, seeing that she educated a group of young female companions to become courtesans. Aeschines says that Lysikles the sheep-dealer, a man lowly born and humble of nature, became the most important man of Athens by living with Aspasia after the death of Perikles. (Plutarch, *Life of Perikles* 34.3-4)

*22.1 Athenian (Attic) red-figure fragment of a kylix (drinking cup), late 6th century B.C. H.: 0.055 m. Athens, Agora Museum P 23133.*

The fragment shows the upper part of a nude woman, probably reclining on cushions at a symposion. She holds a castanet in her left hand and wears disk earrings. She is probably a *hetaira*, or courtesan, a woman accomplished in the arts of music, conversation, and sex.

*22.2 Athenian (Attic) red-figure fragment of a vase, about 460 B.C. H.: 0.057 m. Athens, Agora Museum P 29766.*

In contrast to the hetaira, this woman appears to be a properly dressed Athenian lady. The fragment preserves the upper part of her body and shows us that she wears a tunic, cloak, and headband.

22.5 Attic (Athenian) vase in the form of two heads, 480-460 B.C. [the Princeton Class] H.: 0.149 m. Art Museum, Princeton University 33-45.

This drinking cup is in the form of a white female head and an African male head back to back. Literary texts suggest that the Athenians were interested in the anthropological differences between the two races, so it is not surprising to find them vividly contrasted here and on other vases of this type. The vase has a round mouth and would once have had high handles on each side. The two heads were made in different molds, and all the parts were then joined together. The added colors contrast with the lustrous black glaze: the white of the eyes and of the woman's wreath, the purple of the man's hair, and the red of the lips.

22.3 Terracotta statuette of a woman kneading bread, early 5th century B.C. H.: 0.10 m. Athens, National Archaeological Museum 6006.

The woman is shown in one of her daily occupations, making bread. Many such genre pieces were made in Boiotia, a region close to Attica, and represented such mundane subjects as a carpenter, butcher, barber, or scribe. Women grinding corn, grilling food, or baking bread are also known. Most statuettes of this type were found in tombs and may have been meant to minister to the needs of the dead in the next world.

*22.4 Attic (Athenian) vase in the form of a woman's head, early 5th century B.C. [the Cook Class] H.: 0.15. Athens, National Archaeological Museum 2077.*

The head part of this vase was formed in a mold, while the neck, mouth, rim, and handle were made separately and then attached to the molded portion. Women, Africans, satyrs (the companions of the wine god Dionysos), and occasionally the hero Herakles appear as head vases, which were probably used as jugs to serve wine at a symposion. The trefoil shape of the mouth on this example was well adapted for pouring. The woman's features are rendered in black glaze on the reserved clay ground, with added white and red colors for details. The rows of raised dots on her forehead suggest rows of tight curls across her brow. The rest of her head is covered with lustrous black glaze. Traces of a white wreath are visible on her head.

# 23

## THE UNENFRANCHISED, II - SLAVES AND RESIDENT ALIENS

Also excluded from political participation were two other large segments of the population: slaves and *metics* (resident aliens).

Slavery was common in antiquity, and the Athenians used thousands of slaves in their private homes, factories, and mines, and also as civil servants (23.2). Slaves were usually captured in war and came from all over the Mediterranean, including other Greek cities. Surviving auction records indicate that the prices of slaves varied tremendously, depending on their skills. Despite their unfortunate lot, slaves in democratic Athens were apparently somewhat better off than in other cities, according to one writer of the 5th century B.C.:

Slaves and metics at Athens lead a singularly undisciplined life; one may not strike them there, nor will a slave step aside for you. Let me explain the reason for this situation: if it were legal for a free man to strike a slave, a metic, or a freedman, an Athenian would often have been struck under the mistaken impression that he was a slave, for the clothing of the common people there is in no way superior to that of the slaves and metics, nor is their appearance. There is also good sense behind the apparently surprising fact that they allow slaves there to live in luxury, and some of them in considerable magnificence. ("Xenophon," *Constitution of the Athenians* 1.10-11)

Metics were citizens of other Greek or foreign cities, drawn by the extraordinary opportunities Athens offered to skilled artisans and intelligent businessmen. As in the United States, much of the vitality and energy came from immigrants. They were welcome in Athens, but it was very rare to become a naturalized citizen. Many of the great contributors to Athenian cultural pre-eminence, such as the philosopher Aristotle and the painter Polygnotos, were not Athenian citizens. Many of the craftsmen who built the great temples of the city are known to have been foreigners, and some of the wealthiest business-men and even businesswomen of the city were not Athenian citizens. Whole foreign commu-nities of Egyptians, Cypriots, and Phoenicians sprang up, especially at the port of Piraeus, and they were permitted to establish sanctuaries to their own gods. With foreigners as with slaves, the Athenians were said to be more open than elsewhere:

> This, then, is why in the matter of free speech we have put slaves and free men on equal terms; we have also done the same for metics and citizens because the city needs metics because of the multiplicity of her in-dustries and her fleet; that is why we were right to establish freedom of speech for metics as well. ("Xenophon," *Constitution of the Athenians* 1.12)

Neither slave nor metic played any direct role in the political life of the city; such activity was reserved only for male citizens. Exact figures are hard to come by; however, on any reckoning well under half the total adult population of the city participated in the Athenian democracy.

*23.1 Athenian (Attic) vase in the form of the head of an African, late 6th century B.C. [Class of Boston 00.332]. H.: 0.15 m. Athens, National Archaeo-logical Museum 11725.*

The African racial type was of great interest to the Athe-nians, as this carefully modeled vase indicates. The lustrous black glaze perfected by Athenian potters was well adapted for the subject and may in part explain the popularity of these vases. In this example, the potter has conveyed a sense of the young African's strength. The neck, mouth, and handles of the vase are similar to those used for perfume jars (*aryballoi*), suggesting that this vase might once have held perfumed oil.

*23.2 Athenian (Attic) red-figure kylix (drinking cup),
about 480 B.C., attributed to the painter Onesimos.
H.: 0.09 m. New York, Metropolitan Museum of
Art.*

Africans, like the peoples of many other races captured
in battle, might become slaves in the Athenian state.
Many slaves worked in the fields or silver mines, but
others became domestic servants. Here, an African
groom is shown sighting along his curry comb for hairs
after currying the horse.

*23.3 Athenian (Attic) red-figure plate, 520-510 B.C. Attributed to the painter Paseas. D.: 0.184 m. Oxford, Ashmolean Museum 1879.175 (V.310).*

An archer, carrying a bow, with a combined quiver and bowcase strapped to his waist, rides a horse bareback. His costume may be that of a Skythian, who were a nomadic people inhabiting the shores of the Black Sea. Skythians sometimes signed on as mercenaries in the pay of the Athenian state and so became resident aliens in Athens. The costume consists of embroidered leggings and short jacket, with a soft, animal-skin hat. The inscription on the plate praises Miltiades as beautiful but probably refers to a different Miltiades than the hero of Marathon.

# 24

## SOURCES AND DOCUMENTS

Our understanding of the workings and history of Athenian democracy comes from a variety of sources.

Most useful, perhaps, are the ancient literary texts that survive, many of which have been cited repeatedly in this catalogue. Two works in particular shed light on the Athenian political system: Aristotle's *Athenian Constitution* and pseudo-Xenophon's *Constitution of the Athenians*. Written about 325 B.C., Aristotle's work records the constitutional development of the city over time and then describes the constitution of his own day. Archaeological discoveries in the Athenian Agora have done much to confirm and illuminate his descriptions. The other work, which survives in the writings of Xenophon but which cannot be by him, is also of considerable interest. It was written almost a century before Aristotle and is a much shorter description of the democracy written by an unsympathetic, antidemocratic observer (see Case 17).

An even more direct source than the literary texts are the laws, decrees, treaties, statue bases, and records that the Athenians themselves kept. The democracy, with average citizens holding public offices which changed hands every year, required elaborate and accurate record-keeping. Written on papyrus, lead sheets, and wooden boards, many of these documents were copied onto marble blocks, which survive today (see Cases 1, 3, 4, 6, 8, 10, 16, 18, 21). Some 7,500 inscriptions have been found in the Agora excavations, and over 10,000 more come from other areas of Athens and Attica.

The central archives building of Athens, known as the Metroon because it also housed a sanctuary of the Mother of the Gods (*meter*), contained thousands of documents, now lost. It stood in a central location among the public buildings of the city, next to the Bouleuterion. It overlooked the great open Agora square, just as the National Archives overlooks the Mall in Washington, D.C.

*24.1 Three bone styluses, 2nd-1st century B.C. L.: 0.067-0.127 m. Athens, Agora Museum BI 292, 705, 707.*

The stylus was a writing implement used for scratching letters onto wax tablets. The flat end could be used to smooth the wax and thus erase letters. Important documents or decrees would then be transferred from the impermanent wax to papyrus or stone. Of the materials on which the Athenians wrote, only the stone inscriptions have survived in any quantity.

*24.2 Athenian (Attic) red-figure kylix (drinking cup), 490-480 B.C. D.: 0.21 m. Philadelphia, University Museum 4842.*

The importance of literacy and writing in particular in the young democracy is reflected in the series of 5th century B.C. vases that show youths and boys writing on wax tablets or reciting before a teacher, who checks the accuracy with a wax tablet or papyrus roll. On this cup a young man is seated on a stool writing on a wax tablet held within a wooden case whose lid is open.

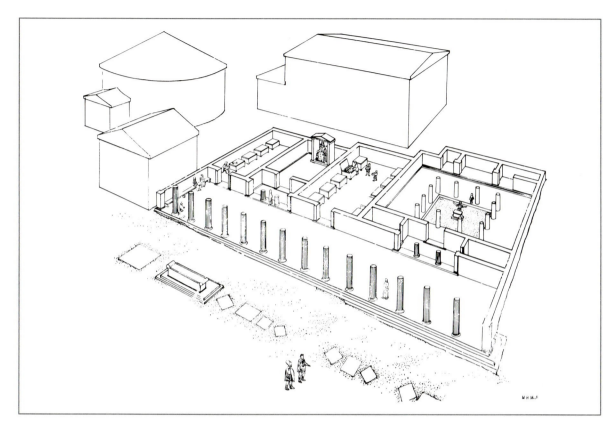

24.3 *The Metroon in the 2nd century B.C. Drawing by Marian H. McAllister.*

The records and decrees of Athens were stored in the Old Bouleuterion (Case 8) where the Boule met during the 5th century B.C. Toward the end of the 5th century, the senate moved to the New Bouleuterion, but the archives stayed behind in the Old Bouleuterion, and the building became known by a new name, the Metroon, named for Rhea, Mother of the Gods, whose cult was also housed in the building. In a speech of Deinarchos against Demosthenes delivered in 323 B.C., we learn that a document was deposited "in the keeping of the Mother of the Gods, who is established as

guardian for the city of all rights recorded in the documents" (*Deinarchos Against Demosthenes* 86). Over fifty such references in the ancient sources describe a full range of documents kept in the building: laws, decrees, records of lawsuits, financial accounts, lists of ephebes, sacred offerings and weights and measures. None of the archives have actually survived, since most of them must have been kept on papyrus or some other perishable material.

The Old Bouleuterion was replaced around 140 B.C. by a larger building consisting of four rooms set side by side, the northernmost a courtyard open to the sky. Across the front of all four rooms, uniting them architecturally, was a colonnade of Ionic columns.

# 25

## THE FOUNDING FATHERS AND ATHENIAN DEMOCRACY

Searching for models for the new government they were creating, America's Founding Fathers studied both the democracy of Athens and the republic of Rome, but they favored the latter. In *The Federalist* essays, James Madison, Alexander Hamilton, and John Jay argued that Athenian democracy was unstable. They thought Athens was too easily ruled by group passion, rather than reason.

*25.1* The Federalist, No. LIV; *by Alexander Hamilton or James Madison. From* The Independent Journal *or the* General Advertiser, *February 13, 1788. Reproduction from the Library of Congress, Washington, DC.*

Had every Athenian citizen been a Socrates, every Athenian assembly would still have been a mob.

To justify the size of the House of Representatives, the author argued against a larger assembly by claiming that in large groups, like the Athenian assembly, "passion never fails to wrest the sceptre from reason."

*25.2* The Federalist, No. LXIII; *by Alexander Hamilton or James Madison. Compilation of essays printed in 1799. The volume was owned by Madison. The Library of Congress, Washington, DC.*

Popular liberty might then have escaped the indelible reproach of decreeing to the same citizens the hemlock on one day and statues on the next.

In support of a 6-year term for Senators, the author cited the misfortune that befalls a government without such continuity. He claims that Athens' short terms of office led to inconsistency and lack of personal accountability.

# 26

## DEMOCRACY FROM THE PAST TO THE FUTURE

Although the Founding Fathers favored the republicanism of ancient Rome over the direct democracy of Athens, they admired the achievements of ancient Athens. Even today, the ideals of Greek democracy influence the way we govern ourselves.

*26.1* Rights of Man *by Thomas Paine. The Library of Congress, Washington, DC.*

What Athens was in miniature America will be in magnitude.

Written in 1792 in defense of the French Revolution, Thomas Paine's *Rights of Man* is a statement of republican ideals. Paine believed that America had adapted the virtues of ancient Greek democracy to the modern world.

*26.2 Senate Joint Resolution 67, 95th Congress. RG 46, Records of the United States Senate, National Archives and Records Administration, page 1.*

Direct initiative, or the right of citizens to propose and vote on legislation, has roots in Greek democracy. In ancient Athens, all decrees had to be ratified by the assembly of citizens before becoming law. In 1977 Senator James Abourezk proposed a constitutional amendment to allow direct initiative nationwide. Many states have some form of direct initiative.

# PERSONIFICATIONS OF DEMOCRACY

## OLGA TZACHOU-ALEXANDRI
### DIRECTOR, NATIONAL ARCHAEOLOGICAL MUSEUM, ATHENS

For all the citizens to be members of the deliberative body and to decide all these matters is a mark of popular government. (Aristotle, *Politics* 4.1298a10).

The poets and artists of ancient Greece gave human form and human traits not only to their gods, but also to abstract concepts, institutions and inanimate objects of the tangible world. Poetic personifications appeared first and inspired the creations of the artists. Each generation personified the concepts of greatest significance to its age. Not surprisingly, the personifications referring to political life originated in fifth century B.C. Athens. The democratization of the Athenian regime began in the last decade of the sixth century B.C. under the enlightened leadership of Kleisthenes (508/7 B.C.). Shortly before the mid-fifth century, it achieved its full potential in the radical reforms of Ephialtes (461 B.C.) and the wise guidance of Perikles (495-429 B.C.), the greatest democratic politician of antiquity.

Thucydides describes the democratic regime as follows (2.37.1):

We have a form of government which does not emulate other peoples' institutions; on the contrary, we are ourselves a model which some follow, rather than the imitators of others. And our government is called a democracy, because its administration is in the hands, not of the few, but of the many. Yet while as regards the law, all citizens are equal for the settlement of their private disputes, as regards the value set on them, it is as each man is in any way distinguished that he is given public honors, not because he belongs to a particular class, but because of personal merits. Nor, again, on the ground of poverty is a man barred from a public career by obscurity of rank if he but wants to render the state a service.

More than ever, the general climate lent itself to the creation of political personifications. In art we encounter the Demos or the "People," the Boule or the "Council," the Democracy and the Oligarchy, i.e. the political organs and the forms of government.

The significance of the Demos was many-sided. In the official sense, the Demos was the sovereign of Attica. Inscriptions mention it, often in close connection with the Boule, as the central decision-making body. The Demos, composed of the assemblies of the people of Attica, claimed to represent the entire population. The Assembly of the Demos, however, governed the Athenian state directly and wielded control over the *archons*. The latter were elected by the Demos and executed its decisions. The meeting place of the Demos was the Pnyx, a hill near the Acropolis dominating the Agora. More than forty times a year, the Athenian citizens gathered on the Pnyx to listen to politicians and leaders of the people before casting their votes. In essence, Athenian politics was fashioned in the Assembly of the Demos on the hill of the Pnyx.

The Boule of Five Hundred consisted of fifty council-members from each of the ten tribes, which represented the inhabitants of the approximately one hundred and forty demes of Attica. The Boule had restricted authority in comparison with the Demos. It drew up the legislative proposals, i.e. the topics and the laws for discussion in the Assembly, and supervised their execution. It was the general coordinator of the functions of state. The building in which the council-members held their meetings, the Bouleuterion, was located on the western side of the Ancient Agora northwest of the Acropolis.

In order to form a general picture of the various possible forms of government in Athens, since these too were personified, we should look for a moment at the prevailing view concerning these forms in the fourth century B.C., as expressed by Aeschines in his oration *Against Ctesiphon*, 6:

> There are three forms of government among the people: tyranny, oligarchy and democracy. Tyranny and oligarchy are administered according to the tempers of their lords, but democratic states according to their own established laws.

It was Demos who was most frequently personified. The earliest relevant sources concern his actual worship. His first sanctuary was founded on the Hill of the Nymphs, a sacred site abutting directly on the Pnyx, the political nucleus of Athenian democracy. According to an inscription carved in the rock, the sanctuary dates back to the middle of the fifth century B.C. The pre-existing sanctuary of the Nymphs was an appropriate location for the worship of Demos: the Nymphs were goddesses of the ordinary citizen;

they guarded the fertility of the land and the people. Another sanctuary of Demos, shared with the Charities, was founded on the northern slope of the Agoraiou Kolonou Hill on the Ancient Agora, the second most important center of political life in Athens. Epigraphical evidence dates its functioning from the third century B.C. The Charites (Graces) allowed for less strict application of the laws of the Demos for humanitarian reasons.

Although the existence of the worship of Demos by the middle of the fifth century B.C. suggests a concurrent personification, the earliest known representations do not date prior to the last quarter of the century. Likewise, the great comic poet Aristophanes employs the personification of Demos in his play *Hippeis*, dating the stage appearance to 424 B.C. From literary sources, we have learned of representations of Demos in painting. This information, however, does not allow us to restore the iconography of Demos, since the monuments mentioned are not sufficiently described. Pliny, a Latin author of the first century A.D., records that the painter Parrhasios was the first to depict Demos at the end of the fifth century B.C. In his work, he tried to convey the volatile character of the Athenian people. Moreover, he represented Demos together with Theseus, the mythical hero of Attica, whom tradition regarded as the founder of Athenian democracy. In his description of the Ancient Agora, Pausanias, a writer and traveler of the second century A.D., mentions that a stoa, now identified as the Stoa of Zeus Eleutherios, housed a wall-painting by Euphranor representing Theseus, Democracy and Demos. This painting, dating from the latter half of the fourth century B.C., was extraordinary for its dynamic portrayal and variety of color, as well as for its political content. It provides the earliest evidence of a deliberate distinction between Democracy as a governmental system and Demos as the sovereign body of Athens. Pliny also informs us about a third pictorial representation, contemporary with the painting by Euphranor, in which Arisolaos depicted Demos, Theseus, and Perikles together. Certainly, this painting was intended to convey a political message.

Literary sources and inscriptions also provide evidence of statues of Demos, which were renowned in the past but are now lost. Pausanias mentions that a statue of Demos made by the fourth century B.C. sculptor Leochares adorned a stoa in Piraeus. The fourth-century orator Demosthenes makes mention of a colossal group representing the Athenian Demos being crowned by the Demoi of Byzantium and Perinthos in accordance with a decree of 340 B.C. Statues of the Demoi of other cities are also known from ancient sources. The tradition of erecting statues of Demos continued through the Roman period.

The so-called decree reliefs are the monuments which constitute our main source for restoring the figure of Demos. These are slabs of stone (stelai) bearing inscriptions crowned with relief representations. Their texts contain official decisions of the People's Assembly. In addition, they provide valuable indications for interpreting and identifying the figures depicted in relief. The figure of Demos is recognizable in approximately twenty-five reliefs. In only four of these can the identification be made with certainty, owing to Demos' name being preserved. Few reliefs are complete; in fact, most are in fragmentary condition. Like the statues, the reliefs represent Demos in one of three functions: as the personification of either the people of Attica, an Attic deme, or the people of another city. Most reliefs portray Demos together with Athena. Only two depict him with

*Figure 1: Decree relief. Athens, National Archaeological Museum 1467.*

the Boule. On one he appears with Eutaxia (the personification of good order) and on another with Democracy.

The earliest representation of Demos can be found on a decree relief in the Louvre Museum (MA831). Its inscription dates from the year 410/9 B.C. and relates to the accounts of the treasury housed in the inner chamber of the Parthenon. Athena and a mature bearded man are portrayed standing on either side of the Sacred Olive Tree. The male figure is identified as the Demos of Athens based upon the responsibilities ascribed to him, including the control and the ratification of the finances. In this relief, the artist employed the sculptural type of the hero of one of the ten Attic tribes, as depicted on the eastern frieze of the Parthenon. These tribal heroes provided the

Figure 2: Decree relief. Athens, Agora Museum I 6524.

Figure 3: Decree relief. Athens, Epigraphical Museum 2811 and 7180.

model for the Attic townsman in sculpture. A decree relief in the National Archaeological Museum (N.M. 1467; see Fig. 1) depicts the Demos of Athens with Athena and the city of Corfu. Demos represents the people of the government concluding a treaty with Corfu in the year 375 B.C.

A decree relief from the Ancient Agora (N. I.6524, see Fig. 2), dating from the archonship of Phrynichos in the year 337/6 B.C., remains the single most important monument for the iconography of Demos. Demos, a mature bearded man, is depicted enthroned. His garment covers his left shoulder, leaving his chest and right shoulder bare. He presumably held a scepter in his left hand. This relief is the only preserved representation of Demos together with Democracy. The distinction between Democracy as a form of government and Demos as the actual governing

body is manifest. This symbolism is also clear from the text of the inscription.

Another relief in the National Archaeological Museum (N.M. 2407) is of particular importance, notwithstanding its worn surface and fragmentary condition: inscriptions identify the three depicted characters as Demos, Athena and Herakles. In this relief, Demos is portrayed seated. The sculpture dates back to the years 340 B.C. The presence of Herakles is justified, since he was the protector of the deme of Melite, where the sculpture was found. Therefore, there is reason to believe that the Demos represented was the local Demos of Melite. A decree relief in the Epigraphical Museum (N. 2811+7180) relates to the Phocians, allies of the Athenians, and dates from 323/2 B.C. (Fig. 3). Demos and Boule, equal in height, are crowning a citizen, who is depicted on a smaller scale. On one side of the relief, Athena, the largest figure of all, is portrayed holding another wreath. A decree relief in the National Archaeological Museum (N.M. 1482, see Fig. 4) presents Euphron of Sicyon, whom Demos is crowning in the presence of Athena. The honored Euphron and his groom are depicted on a smaller scale. This work is dated to 318 B.C. The figure of Demos can also be recognized on another decree relief (N.M. 2958) in the National Archaeological Museum. Here, the presence of Eutaxia is confirmed by an inscription. This relief dates to the decade 320-310 B.C. Representations of Demos crowning a citizen, to honor him for services rendered to the city, are very common. A decree relief in the Museum of Samos (N. I.187), dated between the years 314-306 B.C., is a typical example of Demos representing a Greek city. The Demos of Samos, enthroned, holding a scepter in his left hand, offers a wreath of honor to a middle-aged citizen. Inscribed is the letter Δ, the initial letter of Demos.

These examples compose a representative selection of the various types of reliefs with the figure of Demos. At the same time, they reveal some of his most important characteristics. Most often, Demos is depicted standing, with or without a staff, although sometimes he appears seated on different kinds of seats: a throne, a couch, a theater bench, or a rocky elevation, with or without a scepter, and in various postures. His garment is a himation. He is usually portrayed with a beard. The artists modeled him after the sculptural type of the Attic townsman, although the types of gods such as Asclepios or Zeus are sometimes recognizable.

For the personification of the Boule or for the equivalent local organizations, our information is poor, limited to just three examples, on one of which there is an inscription, "boule." This example, N.M. 1473 (Fig. 5), illustrates an official ceremony or honor granted to a citizen for his service to the city, embodied by Athena herself

*Figure 4: Decree relief. Athens, National Archaeological Museum 1482.*

standing before him. On her right stands "Boule," who is observing or taking part in the ceremony. She is dressed in a chiton and himation, and is similar, iconographically, to female figures we see on contemporary grave stelai.

Our knowledge about the personification of Democracy proves to be much poorer. Even the date of its origin remains uncertain. The personification of Democracy was most likely created in the second half of the fifth century B.C. Evidently, the word "democracy" was not used before the fifth century. It is first mentioned in Herodotus (6.43.3). The first epigraphical evidence of the word, however, is provided by an inscription from the Ancient Agora (N. I.7169, st. 6), dating from the end of the fifth century B.C.

The worship of Democracy was most probably established when the democratic constitution was restored in 403 B.C., after the brief rule and subsequent expulsion of the Thirty Tyrants. At least, this is the conclusion reached by modern research based on historical data as well as epigraphical sources. More specific evidence, however, is available concerning Democracy's worship in Athens in the third century B.C. An inscription on one of the seats of honor in the Theater of Dionysus from the year 224/3 B.C. mentions a priest of Democracy, indicating both the existence and the practice of its worship.

From literary sources, we know of the earliest representations of Democracy. The first reference can be found in a scholiast on the fourth-century orator Aeschines. He records that the funeral monument of Critias (one of the Thirty Tyrants), dating from 403 B.C., depicted Oligarchy, i.e. the regime of the tyrants, setting Democracy on fire with a torch. Unfortunately, the accuracy of this information is questionable. Pausanias provides us with a further, reliable example already mentioned in our description of the monuments representing Demos. It concerns the wall-painting of Euphranor, dating from 340 B.C., in the Stoa of Zeus Eleutherios, which portrayed Theseus, Democracy and Demos. From inscriptions, we know of the existence of at least three statues of Democracy. One statue, a votive offering given by the Council in 333/2 B.C., stood in the Ancient Agora of Athens. Another statue was erected on the island of Salamis before 214/3 B.C. A third adorned the Council-house of Pergamon.

Perhaps the only known decree relief representing Democracy is the above-mentioned stele (Fig. 2) from the Ancient Agora. The text of its inscribed decree identifies the two depicted figures as Demos and Democracy. Democracy, a

*Figure 5: Decree relief. Athens, National Archaeological Museum 1473.*

beautiful woman, is portrayed in a frontal view, standing with her left foot forward. She is dressed in a high-girdled robe and a cloak without emblems. She is crowning Demos with the wreath in her hand. Her comfortable posture and elongated proportions are suitable for a female deity. She can also be compared with the female figures on tombstones, votive offerings, or decree reliefs from the same period. The characters of Democracy and Demos convey the distinction between the form of government and the actual governing body respectively. Aristotle in his

*Politics* (3.1278b9-15) describes it as follows:

> Now a constitution is the ordering of a state in respect of its various magistracies, and especially the magistracy that is supreme over all matters. For the government is everywhere supreme over the state and the constitution is the government. I mean that in democratic states, for example, the people are supreme, but in oligarchies, on the contrary, the few are; and we say that they have a different constitution. And we shall use the same language about the other forms of government also.

Our only information about the personification of Oligarchy is the above-mentioned scholion on Aeschines, which is of doubtful accuracy. The lack of interest in the iconography of Oligarchy clearly shows the unambiguous prejudice of the Athenians against this form of government.

Greece gave birth to Democracy and democratic institutions. This land consequently saw both their personifications and the establishment of their worship. A well-known ancient orator succinctly expresses the Athenian citizen's attachment to the democratic constitution in the following way:

> Our democracy can never be destroyed. We live in harmony with each other, abide by the laws, know how to be steadfast in times of danger and do not abandon the order of freedom.

# A COURT TRIAL IN ATHENS
# EARLY IN THE FOURTH CENTURY B.C.

## ALAN L. BOEGEHOLD
## BROWN UNIVERSITY

Justice at Athens during Archaic and Classical times was administered chiefly in courts that were components of two separate and distinct systems. One system was established for judgments of homicide, as variously defined, and certain related crimes, and its five courts were situated in and around Athens, namely, on the Areopagos, at Palladion, at Delphinion, at Phreatto, and at Prytaneion. Judges sat in panels: in one court they were retired magistrates (200 or so in the Council of the Areopagos) and in others, specially designated officials, 51 in number.

The second system, which can be called "popular," likewise had its final verdicts delivered in four or five courts, all of which were inside the city walls. Almost any offense would be tried in these courts: impiety (for which Sokrates was executed), treason, breaking and entering, cowardice in battle, bribes, embezzlements, in short whatever the city decreed was against the law. Judges sat in large panels numbering not less than 200 and up to 6,000: Athenians had found that a certain critical mass was necessary for a proper verdict. Five hundred, however, is the number of judges most often reported on a panel. Outside these two systems of the homicide and the popular courts, arbitration was widely employed, as were a number of summary procedures.

We know most about the system of popular courts from a treatise written by Aristotle, *The Constitu-* *tion of the Athenians*, and from speeches delivered by Antiphon, Andokides, Isokrates, Lysias, Demosthenes, Aeschines, and other Athenian orators. There survive in addition commentaries on these speeches from later antiquity, and evidence from archaeological excavation by the American School of Classical Studies at Athens. The ancient marketplace, the Agora, has yielded remains of equipment, furniture, and structures that served ancient Athenian judiciary procedures. And so it is now possible to construct in some detail how the trial of Sokrates, to take a very famous instance, might have progressed.

First, Sokrates' accusers, Meletos, Anytos, and Lykon, would have presented themselves at the Royal Stoa, where the King presided (he was not actually a king but one of a dozen or more administrative officers responsible for certain portions of the court calendar). One or all three accusers presented their charge, which was to the effect that Sokrates was corrupting the youth of Athens and introducing strange, new gods into the city.

Once the King agreed that such charges fell within the range of his competence, the prosecutors summoned Sokrates to the Royal Stoa to answer their charges. Sokrates duly arrived and as a result of whatever questioning and answering went on, the King decided that a trial before a panel of 500 judges was called for. He then had a formal notice printed in black paint on a whitened wooden plaque. The notice announced the forthcoming trial in the form of a date (which was the King's responsibility to set) and two oaths, the first of which gave the names of the accusers and their sworn statement of what they believed Sokrates had done wrong, and the second, Sokrates' name and sworn denial. Usually such notices were posted in the Agora, affixed to a railing around the long statue base that held figures of the city's ten eponymous heroes. There, all the people who visited the marketplace would learn abut the coming trial, and many would plan to attend.

On the scheduled day, early in the morning, a mass of would-be judges appeared at an appointed place in the Agora. In order to be eligible, candidates must have been citizens and at least thirty years old and not owe money to the state. They also had to carry a bronze identification tag which had incised or punched into it the owner's name, his father's name, the name of the deme where his citizenship was registered, and his section letter. This last was one of the first ten letters of the alphabet, that is alpha to kappa, and identified a man as belonging to one of ten sections which were created for the purpose of allotting judges to courts. This artificial compartmentalizing of all citizens who had applied for judging services was intended to keep blocks of judges with similar interests from judging together.

The bronze tag not only identified a man as eligible to judge, it also served as an instrument in the allotment that would assign him to a court for the day. At a certain place in the Agora, officials had set up twenty allotment machines, two for each tribe. The allotment machine (or *kleroterion*) was essentially a frame with one bronze tube attached vertically to one side. Its frontal plane,

whether of stone or wood, had vertical rows of slots, each of a size to hold one identification tag. The operation of the allotment was simple. Would-be judges had their tags plugged into the slots. Balls shaken in a container, poured into the top of the tube, were released one at a time from the bottom of the tube. Each ball, by the court name inscribed on it, assigned a horizontal row of would-be judges to a court. On the day in question, suppose that each judging panel was to be composed of 500 judges and the trials were to be held in the Odeion, the Stoa Poikile, and the Parabyston, all sufficiently capacious buildings. A total of 1,500 judges was needed, and so each tribe would supply 150 judges for the day. Upon being assigned to a court, a judge received a staff, which served as the badge of office as he proceeded through the marketplace to his court.

At the trial site, an official monitored entrances, making sure each judge came to the court to which he was allotted. At the same time, he gave out to each judge a bronze token, formed like a coin and carrying a single letter of the alphabet. Distribution was random, and the intent was to assign judges to seating areas by chance. In this way, friends and relations could not sit together and influence proceedings by means of loud, concerted responses. The judges accordingly made their way to a wooden bench within the area designated alpha, beta, or whatever, sat down, and waited for the trial to begin. Outside the court building, kept from entering by a fence or a system of grills between columns of the building, all the interested folk from the marketplace gathered, many of them only curious but some of them committed in one way or another, particularly friends and relations of both parties. And this crowd outside the court area was close enough to the action to be seen and heard. Plato represents himself and other friends of Sokrates as being in a position to see, hear, and be seen and heard.

Prosecutors and the defendant arrived and were seated in front of the judging panel. A herald read aloud the sworn charges and denial, and one of the prosecutors mounted a bema from which he delivered his speech. The prosecution, with a stipulated amount of time in which to convince the judges of its case, could choose either to give all of that time over to one man, or to divide it between the three of them. They could also bring in witnesses. But if they were going to be at all credible, they had to do most of the talking themselves. The time they had was measured by a waterclock, called in Greek *klepsydra* or water-thief. It was a terracotta vessel with a bronze tube leaded into its wall at the base, and an overflow hole up near the top of the wall. The vessel was filled with water, and the bronze tube was stop-pered. As soon as the litigant began to speak, an official in charge of the clock opened the tube, and water began flowing out. When the stipulated amount of water had run out, the speaker's time was up. All trials were timed by waterclock, and no trial lasted longer than a single day. A certain number of liquid measures were given to the pro-secution and an equal number to the defense. Since a man had only a certain amount of time to present his case, he wanted urgently to be able to tell his whole story within the time he was given. It was hardly surprising then that litigants often went to speechwriters for help.

The sequence of a trial like that of Sokrates was as follows: first, the prosecutor spoke, detailing charges. Next, the defendant spoke, denying charges. Either party could produce witnesses and have the secretary read out the laws, testimonies, and oaths. On occasion, a challenge might result in the opening of a sealed vessel called "hedgehog" (*echinos* in Greek). This was a terracotta cooking pot in which texts written on papyrus might be sealed for safekeeping. As soon as the defendant stopped speaking, the judges were issued ballots and asked to vote. The ballots were bronze disks about two inches in diameter with a short tube or peg through the middle. A hollow tube meant a vote to find guilty, a solid peg meant a vote to acquit. A judge took two ballots, one of each sort, and by holding thumb and forefinger over the ends of the tube and peg, he concealed which was which. One by one, all 500 judges deposited in a container the ballot that represented their verdict, the other ballot they dropped in a discard container. When they had all voted, the container with the valid ballots was poured out onto a counting board, where an of-ficial performed the official count. A simple ma-jority of votes determined the verdict, and a tie favored the defendant.

When the defendant had been acquitted, he walked away. This was the end of it. If he was found guilty, and if the city by law required one certain punishment for that particular wrong, the punishment was exacted immediately. If the of-fense, however, was one where judges deter-mined what the guilty party "must pay or have happen to him," then prosecutor spoke from the bema again, arguing for the penalty he thought was due. In Sokrates' case, the prosecutors asked for the death penalty, and as before, their speech was limited in time by the waterclock. Next, the defendant spoke: he proposed in opposition to the prosecutors a penalty that would be less severe but still satisfy the punitive impulses of judges who had just found him guilty. At the end of his presentation, the 500 judges voted again, this time to determine which of the two penalties proposed would be exacted. The penalty was or-dinarily effected immediately.

After the trial, the judges were paid. It was a small amount, about half a day's pay for a skilled or unskilled laborer, but nevertheless meaningful. And there were other incentives for a man to want to judge. The office was a right and privilege of citizenship: It was one way for a man to express himself as a vital participant in the city's life. And a trial was a drama as well. Matters of life and death were determined in those courts. We do not hear of Athenian citizens avoiding jury duty.

# OATHS AND OATHTAKING IN ANCIENT ATHENS

## DINA PEPPA-DELMOUZOU
## DIRECTOR OF THE EPIGRAPHICAL MUSEUM, ATHENS

One of the most important artifacts of Athenian democracy, a large stone block lying on the ground in the Agora of Athens, is represented in this exhibit only by means of a photograph (Case 19.3). The original block rests *in situ* where it served for hundreds of years as the oath-stone of the Athenians. Known simply as the *lithos* ("stone"), it is a large foot-worn slab of limestone three feet wide and ten feet long, which was set on the steps of the Royal Stoa, the headquarters of the archon basileus, chief religious magistrate of Athens. Here all incoming officials swore their oath of office, vowing before the gods, the archon, and the assembled citizens of Athens to uphold the law of the Athenian democracy. Here, too, arbitrators and witnesses at trials were sworn in. Punishment for transgression was a huge fine, sufficient to set up a golden statue to the gods.

The oath was, of course, a moral and religious concept well established in early Greek societies. The penalties for perjury were fearsome: divine vengeance from the gods, often extending through several generations. Punishment for such impiety was left to the Furies (*Erinnyes*), who appear in this context as avengers for forsworn oaths in the earliest extant Greek texts, those of Homer (*Iliad* 19.259) and Hesiod (*Works and Days*, 803-4). Writing in the years around 600 B.C. the poet Alkaios of Lesbos invokes them against the tyrant Pittakos for perjury. Though later Athenian

poets such as Aeschylos and Euripides show the Furies as somewhat more propitious toward men and more lenient toward the guilty, the oath remained an essential element of control over public behavior. From earliest times the oath served as a guarantee that the agreed-upon, established order would prevail.

The verb used for taking an oath, *tamnein* or *temnein* (to cut), indicates that the procedure required the sacrifice of animals and the cutting of the victims into pieces, which were offered to the participants. This custom appears all over the Greek world from Homeric times (*Iliad* 2.124, 3.105, 4.155) until at least the fourth century B.C. That this is the type of oath sworn at the *lithos* in the Agora is specifically attested by Pollux (8.86), who wrote in the second century A.D., "They took the oath near the Royal Stoa, on the stone on which were the parts (*tomia*) of the victims, swearing that they would guard the laws."

The fourth-century orator Lykourgos provides the most explicit account of the importance of the oath in Athenian public life, referring to it as the "mortar of Democracy" ( *vs. Leokrates* 79). In his speech, Lykourgos indicates that the participants in all three branches of the government, executive (archons), judiciary (arbitrators and jurors), and legislative (private citizens), swear allegiance to their city by means of the oath. It is clear that such oaths must have been a necessary bond holding together the diverse elements of Athenian society.

The 500 citizens who made up the *boule* (senate) were appointed annually by lot and swore to respect the laws of Solon, to consider the best for the *demos* (people), and to allow no unworthy *bouleutes* (senator) to be admitted the following year. Other provisions of the bouleutic oath are known, referred to in the speeches of orators and preserved in a fragmentary inscription (*IG* I2 114). The *archons* (magistrates) took the bouleutic oath as well. After taking the oath in the Agora, they went in procession up to the Acropolis, where they repeated the oath, swearing before the statue of Athena Polias. After the oath they were crowned with myrtle branches, an act symbolizing their assumption of power.

The jurors who made up Athenian lawcourts were chosen from 5,000 who had been sworn in for the year (Demosthenes 23.78). These 5,000 jurymen, plus 1,000 substitutes, were chosen by lot from among all those citizens who were over thirty years old. The selection was made by means of a special allotment machine (*kleroterion*, Case 11), which was also used on occasion for selecting the boule or other magistrates. The largest popular court was known as the *Heliaia* and the oath taken, dating back to the sixth century B.C., is preserved in a speech of Demosthenes (*vs. Timokrates* 149):

### The Oath of the Heliasts

I will give verdict in accordance with the statutes and decrees of the People of Athens and of the Council of Five Hundred. I will not vote for tyranny or oligarchy. If any man try to subvert the Athenian democracy or make any speech or any proposal in contravention thereof, I will not comply. I will not allow private debts to be canceled, nor lands nor houses belonging to Athenian citizens to be redistributed. I will not restore exiles or persons under sentence of death. I will not expel, nor suffer another to expel, persons here resident in contravention of the statutes and decrees of the Athenian People or of the Council. I will not confirm the appointment to any office of any person still subject to audit in respect of any other office, to wit the offices of the nine Archons or of the Recorder or any other office for which a ballot is taken on the same day as for the nine Archons, or the office of Marshal, or ambassador, or member of the Allied Congress. I will not suffer the same man to hold the same office twice, or two offices in the same year. I will not take bribes in respect of my judicial action, nor shall any other man or woman accept bribes for me with my knowledge by any subterfuge or trick whatsoever. I am not less than thirty years old. I will give impartial hearing to prosecutor and defendant alike, and I will give my verdict strictly on the charge named in the prosecution. The juror shall swear by Zeus, Poseidon, and Demeter, and shall invoke destruction upon himself and his household if he in any way transgress this oath, and shall pray that his prosperity may depend upon his loyalty to it.

Unlike many others, this oath was taken on Ardettos Hill, outside the city walls, to the southeast of Athens.

The speech of Lykourgos against Leokrates preserves other examples of the use of the oath, such as that sworn by the military recruits or *ephebes*, who swore to obey their orders, maintain their ranks, and to fight bravely for their native city (*vs. Leokrates* 77):

The Oath - I will not bring dishonor on my sacred arms nor will I abandon my comrade wherever I shall be stationed. I will defend the rights of gods and men and will not leave my country smaller, when I die, but greater and better, so far as I am able by myself and with the help of all. I will respect the rulers of the time duly and the existing ordinances duly and all others which may be established in the future. And if anyone seeks to destroy the ordinances I will oppose him so far as I am able by myself and with the help of all. I will honor the cults of my fathers. Witnesses to this shall be the gods Agraulus, Hestia, Enyo, Enyalius, Ares, Athena the Warrior, Zeus, Thallo, Auxo, Hegemone, Herakles, and the boundaries of my native land, wheat, barley, vines, olive-trees, fig-trees.

In addition to these examples of oaths used to ensure stability and harmony within the state, the oath was used also to help regulate relations between the various Greek city-states. Before the battle of Plataia, for instance, the Greeks swore a common oath vowing eternal hatred for the Persians and promising not to rebuild any of the ruined temples, but to leave them as permanent reminders of barbarian impiety (Lykourgos, *vs. Leokrates* 81).

The Athenian empire of the fifth century B.C. was held together by a network of alliances and treaties, all sealed by oaths. A forsworn oath was ample legal reason for action against a recalcitrant ally, as the people of Euboia learned in 446 B.C., when they rebelled against Athens, drawing upon themselves a military expedition led by Perikles. Later, after the collapse of the empire following the Peloponnesian War, the Athenians made a new series of individual treaties with Boiotia (395 B.C.), Eretria (394 B.C.), Byzantium (378 B.C.), and Methymna (377 B.C.). In 377 B.C. the so-called Naval League was established; the charter between Athens and 75 other states is preserved and stands today in the Epigraphical Museum (*IG* II2, 43), as do all the above-mentioned individual treaties. The alliance was sworn to by generals, cavalry commanders, and members of the council for each of the signatory states and contains the Greek phase for "forever." This same oath-taking ceremony is attested in 356 B.C. between Philip II of Macedon and the Chalcidic League. Specific punishments are listed as well for any magistrate or citizen who went against the alliance and his word. The perjurer was to be banished from all confederate territory or put to death, in which case he could not even be buried in any confederate land.

Ancient sources indicate that other cities, too, had specific stones at which oaths were taken. Pausanias (VIII. 15) describes such an oath-stone (*petroma*) in the Arcadian city of Pheneos:

> Beside the sanctuary of the Eleusinian goddess is what is called the Petroma, two great stones fitted to each other. Every second year, when they are celebrating what they call the Greater Mysteries, they open these stones, and taking out of them certain writings which bear on the mysteries, they read them in the hearing of the initiated, and put them back in their place that same night. I know, too, that on the weightiest matters most of the Pheneatians swear by the Petroma.

The reference to Eleusinian Demeter reminds us of the religious aspect of oath-taking and also turns our attention back to Attica, to the sanctuary of Demeter at Eleusis, whose rites were adopted by the people of Pheneos. Here, too, there is a pair of boulders which fit closely together leaving a secret compartment deep within. This unusual installation lies in a prominent spot, on the right of the Sacred Way as one approaches the Telesterion (Hall of Mysteries) from the north.

Finally, when appearing before the Areopagos homicide court in Athens, litigants stood on two stones according to Pausanias (I. 28). "The unwrought stones on which the accused and accusers stand are named respectively, the stone of Injury and the stone of Ruthlessness."

As noted, the location of the *lithos* in the Agora makes clear its significance in the political life of Athens. It rests on the steps of the Royal Stoa (Case 19), headquarters of the King Archon. This magistrate held important legal and religious responsibilities, inherited from the old kingship (Aristotle, *Athenian Politics* 57). On the walls of the stoa and on stelai standing nearby were displayed inscribed copies of the ancient laws of Draco and Solon, the very ones the archons of Athens swore to uphold. If the oath was indeed the mortar of democracy, then the *lithos* must surely be understood as the cornerstone on which the Athenian democracy was founded.

# ATHENIAN DEMOCRACY DENOUNCED: THE POLITICAL RHETORIC OF AMERICA'S FOUNDERS

JENNIFER ROBERTS
CITY UNIVERSITY OF NEW YORK

Men and women of eighteenth-century America inevitably approached the world with the face of Janus. An uncertain future lay before them, and much of what they would make of that future depended on how they chose to interpret the dead certainties of the past. Yet what the past had to teach them was neither dead nor certain. What they thought they knew about the classical world was really a drama, often a morality play, that had been composed over centuries by a combination of oral and written traditions that left ancient realities far behind.

Where Athens was concerned, America's founders were privy to a long tradition that emphasized the weaknesses of the democratic system. Moreover, their own fears for the sanctity of property in an age of unrest made them easily frightened by specters of unruly masses confiscating and redistributing the goods of the rich. John Adams was convinced that this had really happened in Athens. Adams's revulsion for any form of redistribution of wealth led him to deny that the revered Athenian liberator Solon, long hailed as the savior of the poor because of his cancellation of debts and abolition of debt slavery, had in fact done the things for which he was justly famous. Other fears came into play as well—the fear of instability and of the tyranny of the

majority. Centuries of writing about Athens tended to reinforce all these apprehensions.

The tradition America's founders encountered when they turned to the classical past had built up for over two thousand years. The notion that there was something radically amiss with the Athenian democracy had originated in Athens itself among wealthy intellectuals—men whose families in a nondemocratic state would have been accorded special privileges denied ordinary people. Thucydides, for example, in his history of the Peloponnesian War, stressed the volatility of the masses, their emotionality, and their susceptibility to flattery. Xenophon, who took up Thucydides' narrative where it had been left when Thucydides died, was an admirer of Sparta. He believed that people who worked for a living at dreary trades should not be allowed to participate in civic life. (The Spartans had "solved" this problem by a tripartite division of society into citizen-warriors, agricultural serfs, and free but disenfranchised artisans.) Plato shared Xenophon's admiration for Sparta, and the belief that unpleasant manual labor was incompatible with the mental development necessary for good citizens was seconded by Aristotle, who made it a cornerstone of his view of the good life.

A number of sensational court trials also fed the negative tradition about Athenian democracy: the execution of Sokrates took place only a few years after six Athenian generals were put to death for failing to retrieve sailors from choppy waters after a stunning naval victory, even though some accounts maintain that the sailors were dead already and simply required proper burial. And when the Athenians failed to respond adequately to the threats posed to their independence by Philip, the unscrupulous king of Macedonia, they threw themselves open to still another calumny.

What the Athenians had sought to do was actually quite remarkable: to create a cohesive, dynamic community in which most voters would hold office at least once in their lives, trial by jury would replace arbitration by aristocratic judges, and decision making would lie with large groups rather than a few powerful individuals. But by the fourth century B.C. the antidemocratic tradition had already begun to take on a life of its own. In the insightful first pages of his book *The Crowd and the Mob*, J. S. McClelland calls attention to the seminal role of democracy in bringing to birth the political theory of the West. The original purpose of political theory, he maintains, was in fact to show why democracy cannot work, and the impossibility of democracy was to become something of a hobby horse for defensive political analysts for centuries after the failure of the Athenian experiment—or, rather, one should say, after the defeat of the Athenian armed forces by those of Macedon in 338 B.C. For Athenian democracy as a system did not in fact fail; what happened was simply that the Athenians of the later fourth century made several bad judgments about how best to deal with Philip. It is peculiar that the military defeat of Athens by the extraordinary machinations of a determined ruler of a large and wealthy kingdom should have been taken by

historians and political theorists as proof that Athenian democracy did not work, and sometimes even as proof that democracy in general does not work.

To the reservations of Greek intellectuals were added those of several influential Romans. Cicero, for example, when exiled from Rome, had exulted in comparing himself to Athens' martyred statesmen, who (he thought) had been unappreciated by rude and untutored folk. Plutarch, an eminently class-conscious writer of the Roman imperial period, viewed Athenian politics as a running battle between cultivated statesmen of vision and vulgar, short-sighted voters. During the Middle Ages, few people thought very hard about Athenian democracy, a political system extraordinarily alien to the hierarchic cast of mind that characterized medieval thinkers. But during the Italian Renaissance new interest was focused on the city-states of ancient Greece, and what thinkers like Machiavelli and Guicciardini had to say about Athens would have great influence on America's founders. Identifying Athens with commercial Florence, Machiavelli and Guicciardini praised instead the stability of Sparta and maintained that Athens, like all popular states, was hopelessly fragile and vulnerable.

Although in reality the differences between classical Athens and Renaissance Florence were enormous, for centuries thinkers from many nations—Italy, France, Switzerland, Germany, England, and the United States, to name just a few—focused on the similarities between the two cities, stressing above all the leading place each one occupied in the intellectual life of its time. But in fact the intense competition of the Florentine guilds and the meteoric speed with which fortunes were made and lost in that banking city makes Athens look like a peaceful farming village by contrast. The Athenian state was actually remarkably stable; indeed twentieth-century writers, less preoccupied with the specter of instability than their predecessors of the eighteenth, often remark on the stability of classical Athens. But the connection that Renaissance thinkers drew between Athenian and Florentine instability were very real in their own minds, and this link made a deep impression on eighteenth-century readers, who were convinced that parallels and analogies made history somehow universal and endowed it with timeless relevance.

In sum, the tradition that America's founders inherited about Athens was distinctly hostile, and by and large the Athenian example was one from which they were eager to disassociate themselves and their new republic. In *Federalist Paper* no. 14, for example, James Madison was careful to distinguish between the promising republics of the United States on the one hand and the "turbulent democracies of ancient Greece" on the other. The representative principle, he contended, would protect Americans against the perils of the direct democracy of the Athenians; a well-constructed senate would provide security from the "artful misrepresentations of interested men" and save the citizens of the United States from the pitfalls of Athenian-style democracy. Like many who went before him and many who would come after, Madison appealed to the example of Sokrates in condemning the Athenians for their volatility. "What bitter anguish," he asked, "would not the people of Athens have often escaped if their government had contained so provident a safeguard against the tyranny of their own passions? Popular liberty might then have escaped the indelible reproach of decreeing to the same citizens the hemlock on one day and statues the next." Similar arguments were put forward by Alexander Hamilton, who contrasted his own new nation, the beneficiary of a system of checks and balances, with those of antiquity, contending that Greek states (except Sparta) offered only a history that "no friend to order or to rational liberty can read without pain and disgust."

The superiority of American republicanism to Athenian democracy was frequently put forward by John Adams, whose works made plain that he had a large amount of enthusiasm for a small amount of democracy. In Athens, he contended, "factious demagogues" often egged the people on to their own destruction, and the instability he perceived in Athenian government led him to inquire, in a sentence that stood alone as a paragraph,

Is this government, or the waves of the sea?

Adams was also convinced that the Athenian democrats habitually violated the sanctity of property, and the glaring absence of evidence for this contention did not discourage him from persisting in his belief. Majority rule, he concluded, would entail "the eight or nine millions who have no property . . . usurping over the rights of the one or two million who have." Debts, he feared, "would be abolished first; taxes laid heavy on the rich, and not at all on the others; and at last a downright equal division of every thing be demanded, and voted." Adams was far from alone in his anxieties. The records of the Federal Convention of 1787 make plain that Adams's concern with private property was shared by many of his American peers. The notion that Athenians habitually violated the sanctity of property also formed an important building block in the antidemocratic arguments of the Englishman William Mitford, whose *History of Greece* was composed throughout the 1780s and 1790s. "The satisfaction . . . of an Englishman," Mitford wrote, "in considering his house and his field more securely his own, under the protection of the law, than a castle defended by its own garrison, or a kingdom by its armies," was "unknown" in Athens, where the nobility were forced to "cringe" to the rabble in order to protect their property. In Athens, he insisted, "property, liberty, and life itself were incomparably less secure" than under the "mild firmness" of the "mixed government" of Britain.

Although Adams was a staunch republican and Mitford a committed monarchist, the two men were united in their conviction that the best form of government was a mixed state in which power followed property, and on the whole Adams spoke for most federalists in his rejection of the Athenian model. The repeated stress the founders placed on the inadequacies—real or perceived—of the Athenian democracy reveals much about their apprehensions concerning popular government. A good deal can be learned from the pronounced parallels between the writings of two men as different as the English Mitford and the American Adams. In assessing the foundation of the American republic, it is important not to lose sight of the founders' preoccupation with the rights of the propertied classes and their desire to protect their own class against the encroachments of the ordinary citizen. Their shared conviction that the best rhetorical use of classical Athens was as an admonitory counterexample provides a crucial reminder that republicanism and egalitarianism do not necessarily go hand in hand.

SUGGESTED READING

F. Adams, ed., *The Works of John Adams, Second President of the United States*, Boston 1856; quotations from vol. 4, pp. 480-485 and vol. 6, p. 9

A. Hamilton, *Papers*, ed. H. Syrett, New York 1961; quotation from vol. 2, p. 657

J. S. McClelland, *The Crowd and the Mob: From Plato to Canetti*, New York 1989

W. Mitford, *History of Greece*, London 1822 edition; quotations from vol. 5, pp. 31, 34; vol. 3, p. 4; vol. 5, p. 219

C. Rossiter, ed., *The Federalist Papers*, New York and Scarborough, Ontario 1961; quotations from pp. 100, 384

E. Sagan, *The Honey and the Hemlock*: *Democracy and Paranoia in Ancient Athens and Modern America*, New York 1991

# ATHENIAN DEMOCRACY IDEALIZED: NINETEENTH-CENTURY PHOTOGRAPHY IN ATHENS

## ANDREW SZEGEDY-MASZAK
## WESLEYAN UNIVERSITY

"We are all Greeks," the poet Shelley proclaimed. The scholars, travelers, and artists of the nineteenth century crafted an idealized image of ancient Greece, or more specifically of Classical Athens, whose essential nature was depicted as an amalgam of democratic freedom, literary genius, intellectual adventurousness, and aesthetic sophistication. It was this vision that Shelley was invoking, and although it has been sharply revised by subsequent scholars and historians, it remains influential. In the following pages I shall briefly consider two linked features of nineteenth-century cultural history: the "rediscovery of Greece," as expressed in the comments of foreign visitors, and its reflection in the then-new medium of photography. In this period, imagery and ideology were combined to celebrate Athenian democracy.

In the nineteenth century, Greek antiquity gradually replaced Roman antiquity as the area for advanced study of the Classics and, more broadly, as the model for aesthetic and political debate. The Greek war of independence against Turkey (1821-1829) had drawn enthusiastic support from European philhellenes, the most famous of whom was Lord Byron. After the war the country became much more accessible to travelers from Western Europe and was particularly attractive to visitors from Britain and France. Partly due to

Byron's passionate verses, the ideal of democracy, often conveyed in the term "liberty," suffused Attica in the minds of travelers.

The resurgence of interest in Greece was not due solely to political developments. Throughout the nineteenth century, and indeed until World War I, classical studies dominated higher education in England and the Continent. As a result the Classical texts constituted the single most significant influence on both the writers and the photographers of Athens. Every important place resonated with echoes of the glorious past. J. P. Mahaffy, an Irish classicist who published an account of his travels in Greece in the mid-1870s, voiced typical sentiments:

> As to Cicero the whole land was one vast shrine of hallowed memories—*quocumque incedis, historia est* [wherever you go, there is history]—so to the man of culture this splendor of associations has only increased with the lapse of time and the greater appreciation of human perfection.

Although Athens was undergoing enormous social and political change, foreign travelers found the shades of antiquity much more engaging than modern realities.

For a long time, travel narratives had been accompanied by different kinds of illustrations, which travelers could use to enhance their memories and nontravelers could enjoy vicariously. Books and journals were illustrated with sketches, or reproductions thereof, and most of the eminent tourist sites were immortalized in mass-produced prints and engravings that could be bought on site or ordered by mail. Photography, invented in 1839, brought a wholly new standard of realism to the world of visual representation. For their nineteenth-century audience, photographs seemed miraculously true to life and free from the embellishments of artistic fancy. Despite their seeming objectivity, however, the photographs of classical sites were shaped by the same conventions that governed the travelers' stories. Neither genre, for example, shows much interest in scientific archaeology, in the social history of the ancient city, or in the nuances of architecture or engineering. Instead, the visitors' quest was for experiences that would conform to their sense of what was "essentially Greek." The photographers, especially those professionals whose pictures were meant for purchase by travelers, produced images that corresponded to the wishes of their clients.

With its splendid monuments and rich history, Athens occupied the pinnacle of the classical ideal. In addition it offered a wonderfully simple itinerary, because most of the monuments were centrally located, on or next to the Acropolis. A few places within easy traveling distance of the city—Sounion, Eleusis, Marathon—also became part of every educated visitor's experience. These noble ruins and heroic sites acquired iconic status as embodiments of Greek tradition, and they became mandatory stops for visitors and subjects for photographers. A photograph, of course, can never literally depict an abstraction such as democracy. When, however, we consider photographs together with contemporary travelers' accounts, we can see how they interacted in the construction of an ideal of Greek antiquity, in which democracy played a crucial role.

## MARATHON

"The battle of Marathon, as an event in English history, is more important than the battle of Hastings." John Stuart Mill (1846)

Late in 490 B.C., on the plain of Marathon, which lies about twenty miles northeast of Athens, a small Greek force composed of Athenians and a handful of allied troops, under the command of the Athenian general Miltiades, confronted a vastly larger Persian army that had been dispatched by King Xerxes. Although we cannot reconstruct the course of the battle, the result was unequivocal. In a complete reversal of what everyone had expected, the Greeks won a victory that stunned their opponents. The historian Herodotus claims that the Persians lost 6,400 men, while the Greek casualties numbered only 192. The figures, particularly as regards the Persians, are almost certainly exaggerated, and although the Persians were forced to retreat, the actual damage to their empire was negligible. In purely military terms, the engagements at Salamis and Plataea during the second invasion ten years later, were much more significant. Nonetheless, the victory at Marathon immediately catapulted Athens into the first rank of Greek city-states and became a powerful, prideful feature of the Athenians' self-definition and self-esteem. The democracy that had been radically reshaped by Kleisthenes was not yet twenty years old, yet it was democracy itself that was credited with providing the spirit that enabled the greatly outnumbered Greeks to mount a successful defense of their homeland. While the Persians were subjects of a king and

*Figure 1: View of Marathon. Photographer unknown,
1870's. Private collection.*

fought under compulsion, the Greeks were free men who had made the independent choice to defend their freedom.

In the imagination of the West, Marathon came to symbolize the triumph of liberty over despotism, and for the nineteenth-century traveler the site was charged with memories of past glory. The power of imaginative projection—or, to be more succinct, historical fantasy—is evident in the visual imagery. The plain was a barren spot, covered with scrub and a few straggling trees. Its only distinguishing feature was the great central tumulus, or burial mound, that had been heaped up over the Athenian dead and had been crowned with the statue of a lion. The statue disappeared long ago, and the site was otherwise undistinguished. Nonetheless, travelers saw not the bleak present but the splendor of antiquity. A typical reaction is expressed by Christopher Wordsworth, who visited Marathon in 1832 and said of the tumulus, "No one can find himself alone with an object like this and not feel a sense of awe."

Photographers could rely on such associations to infuse their images with a resonance they would otherwise lack. The historical overtones were especially salient here because the location had none of the elements of the picturesque or the sublime, no towering peaks, rushing waterfall or imposing ruins. In the 1870s an anonymous commercial photographer produced a view (Fig. 1) that was bought by a British traveler, who carefully mounted it in a lavish album, alongside many photographs more interesting and more beautiful. This picture is standard topographical fare. It predictably includes, for example, a small figure near the top of the tumulus to give some idea of scale. As a picture it is dull and not very informative, but its original owner endowed it with depth of meaning and symbolic value simply by penciling in a caption underneath it: "Marathon." The name was enough.

## THE ACROPOLIS

"From the gates of the Acropolis, as from a mother city, issued intellectual colonies into every region of the world. These buildings now before us, ruined as they are at present, have served for two thousand years as models for the most admired fabrics in every civilized country of the world. Having perished here, they survive there." Christopher Wordsworth (1860)

"The specific quality of the Athenian landscape is light . . . luminous beauty, serene expanse to the air of heaven. The Acropolis is the centre of this landscape, splendid as a work of art with its crown of temples." J. A. Symonds (1879)

Both topographically and metaphorically, the great limestone plateau of the Acropolis represented Athens at its height. Under the rule of the Peisistratid tyrants in the sixth century B.C., it became the site of the most prominent temples for the Athenian community, in particular those devoted to the patron goddess, Athena. During the second Persian invasion in 480 B.C., the sacred buildings on the Acropolis were destroyed along with much of the rest of the city.

After the Persians had once again been driven off, this time for good, the triumphant city-state strode on a path of expansion and domination. Its leader was the brilliant aristocrat Perikles, who fostered the twin policies of radical democracy at home and aggressive imperialism abroad. In the early 440s Perikles proposed that the Athenians use surplus funds they had accumulated from "tribute" paid by Greek allies to beautify the city.

Figure 2: *The western facade of the Propylaea, with the Temple of Victory and the ancient steps. William James Stillman, 1870, Carbon print. 18.4 x 24.3 cm. Malibu, J. Paul Getty Museum 84.XO.766.4.7.*

*Figure 3: Athens - Acropolis from the southwest with the Odeion of Herodes Atticus. Dimitrios Constantin, 1865, Albumen print. 28.4 x 38.7 cm. Malibu, J. Paul Getty Museum 84.XM.366.2.*

Despite objections from political opponents, who complained that he was dressing up the city like a high-priced harlot, Perikles' building plan went forward, employing the most renowned and skillful architects, sculptors, and artisans.

On the Acropolis there rose a magnificent set of buildings. The Propylaea was an elaborate entryway that contained a gallery to display paintings (Fig. 2). Once the visitors had passed through the Propylaea, they found themselves in a thicket of statues and altars, above which soared the Par-

thenon, the massive, richly decorated temple of Athena. Some two decades later, in the late 420s, the Athenians were engaged in the long and ultimately ruinous war with Sparta. Nonetheless they undertook construction of the last major buildings on the Acropolis, one of which was the small, elegant temple dedicated to Athena Nike (Victory), located on the parapet adjoining the Propylaea. At the same time they began work on the Erechtheion, an ancient shrine, now completely rebuilt, that housed the cults of Athena and Poseidon and the hero Erechtheus, who gave

*Figure 4: Parthenon, from the northwest. Petros Moraites,*
*1870, Albumen print. 37.3 x 50.5 cm. Malibu,*
*J. Paul Getty Museum 85.XM.368.1.*

the building his name. In the centuries that followed, the Acropolis underwent substantial changes, under the pressure of war, religion, politics, and both worshipful and hostile looting. Despite such destructive alterations, nineteenth-century travelers regarded the Acropolis as the physical embodiment of the genius of the Athenian polis during the democratic "Golden Age." The ruined condition of the monuments only added to their allure. After a visit on a moonlit night, even Mark Twain, whose *Innocents Abroad* appeared in 1869, abandons his usual wry detachment and declares that the Acropolis contains "the noblest ruins we had ever looked upon."

J. F. Young published his account of his *Five Weeks in Greece* in 1876, and he sums up the feelings of most travelers as they approached the city from the port in Piraeus: "Soon we found ourselves in the outskirts of the modern city; while Ancient Athens . . . looked down on us from the Acropolis and demanded all our attention." The photographs that replicate such sentiments are the long views, like the one by the Athenian photographer Constantine (Fig. 3). They are generally taken from the southwest and show the Acropolis dominating the landscape. Remarkably enough, they succeed in including most of the monuments on and around the Acropolis while at the same time eliminating almost all signs of the small modern city. Although the Parthenon and its neighbors are tiny in such pictures, the images provide a sense of completeness: here, neatly gathered together, are all the things one should see. Moreover, the absence of detail, combined with the virtual disappearance of modern elements, gives free rein to the viewer's imagination. Such an image is much like the first glimpse of a long-sought destination. This miniature stage set is "Athens," and if approached in the right frame of mind, it could come back to life. So

thought Twain: "The place seemed alive with ghosts. I half expected to see the Athenian heroes of twenty centuries ago glide out of the shadows and steal into the old temple they knew so well and regarded with such boundless pride."

THE PARTHENON

> "In spite of all that has befallen it . . . the Parthenon lives forever, and rises above its own decay, for it has the prestige of its former glory, and the sympathy and admiration of the civilized world." J. F. Young (1876)

If, as Symonds claimed, the Acropolis was the crown of Athens, the Parthenon was the preeminent jewel in that crown. Begun in 447, it was the first project in the Periklean building program. The temple's architecture is a masterpiece of the severe Doric style, here deployed with an almost inconceivable degree of refinement. It also had an elaborate program of sculptural decoration. Taken all together, the sculptures encapsulated some of the most significant features of Athenian civic ideology. The exterior elements emphasized the importance of struggle in the creation and maintenance of order, while the great frieze that ran around the interior symbolized harmony and civic unity. By the time the nineteenth-century travelers saw the Parthenon, not only had it been the victim of a calamitous explosion (in 1687), but it had also been stripped of most of its sculpture. No matter. It could still inspire rapturous reflections.

Most photographs were taken from the west end (Fig. 4). Although this was actually the back of the temple, it was the first view a visitor saw after entering the sacred precinct, and more important, it was relatively the best preserved. Although there remained only one battered remnant of its original sculptural group, the triangular pediment

*Figure 5: Western portico of the Parthenon. William James
Stillman, 1870, Carbon print. 24.3 x 19.1 cm.
Malibu, J. Paul Getty Museum 84.XO.766.4.11.*

retained much of its outline, so that this facade came closest to evoking the experience of ancient times. In order to include the complete structure, moreover, the photographers had to stay a certain distance away, so that the pictures convey some of the deferential respect the monument inspired. Edward Lear wrote to his sister in 1848, "No words can give any idea of the appearance of such a vast mass of gigantic ruins all of dazzling white marble, of the most exquisite proportions." Seen from the west—a view that also emphasized its eminence on the highest point of the Acropolis —the Parthenon seemed to exemplify balance, rationality, order, and clarity. In other words, its "exquisite proportions" epitomized the conception of ancient Athens that travelers brought with them.

One final image will make the connection even clearer. The American artist William James Stillman had studied painting with the famous critic John Ruskin and had founded *The Crayon*, the first serious American art journal. Stillman then turned to a career in diplomacy. After a brief stay in Rome, he began to serve as consul in Crete in 1866 but was forced to leave when he supported a Cretan uprising against Turkish rule. After moving to Athens, he made a brilliant series of photographs of the Acropolis and its monuments, which were published in London in 1870. Among the most unusual is his study of the interior of the western portico of the Parthenon (Fig. 5). The evocative use of deep perspective and dramatic lighting highlights one detail, as he notes in his caption: "The names scratched on the columns are those of Philhellenes, who fought here in the war of Greek independence." Stillman, who had so recently championed another struggle for liberation, has crafted an image whose allegorical content is explicit and unmistakable. In his photograph of the columns of Parthenon, the monument of Periklean democracy becomes a memorial, and an inspiration, to the modern defenders of freedom.

# BIBLIOGRAPHY

We include here a list of some recent, and some classic, works in English on the history and archaeology of Athenian democracy which you may wish to look up for additional information.

Camp, John McK., *The Athenian Agora: Excavations in the Heart of Classical Athens*, London 1986.

Cohen, David, *Law, Sexuality, and Society: The Enforcement of Morals in Classical Athens*, Cambridge 1992.

Connor, W.R., *The New Politicians of Fifth-Century Athens*, Princeton 1971.

Dahl, Robert A., *Democracy and Its Critics*, New Haven 1989.

Davies, J.K., *Democracy and Classical Greece*, London 1978.

Ehrenberg, Victor, *From Solon to Socrates*, 2nd ed., London 1973.

Finley, M.I., *Democracy Ancient and Modern*. 2nd ed. New Brunswick, NJ 1985.

—, Politics in the Ancient World, Cambridge 1983.

Forrest, W.G., *The Emergence of Greek Democracy: The Character of Greek Politics, 800-400 B.C.*, London 1966.

Hansen, M.H., *The Athenian Democracy in the Age of Demosthenes: Structure, Principles and Ideology*, Oxford 1991.

Hignett, C., *History of the Athenian Constitution to the End of the Fifth Century B.C.*, Oxford 1952.

Jones, A.H.M., *Athenian Democracy*, Oxford 1957.

Just, Roger, *Women in the Athenian Law and Life*, London and New York 1989.

Kagan, Donald, *Pericles of Athens and the Birth of Democracy*, New York 1990.

Keuls, Eva, *The Reign of the Phallus: Sexual Politics in Ancient Athens*, New York 1985.

Manville, P.B., *The Origins of Citizenship in Ancient Athens*, Princeton 1990.

Meier, Christian, *The Greek Discovery of Politics*, Translated by D. McLintock, Cambridge, Mass. 1990.

Murray, Oswyn, *Early Greece*, London 1980.

Murray, Oswyn, and Simon Price, eds., *The Greek City from Homer to Alexander*, Oxford 1990.

Ober, Josiah, *Mass and Elite in Democratic Athens: Rhetoric, Ideaology, and the Power of the People*, Princeton 1989.

Osborne, Robin, *Demos: The Discovery of Classical Attika*, Cambridge 1985.

Ostwald, Martin, *From Popular Sovereignty to the Sovereignty of Law: Law, Society, and Politics in Fifth-century Athens*, Berkeley and Los Angeles 1986.

—, *Nomos and the Beginnings of the Athenian Democracy*, Oxford 1969.

Patterson, Orlando, *Freedom in the Making of Western Culture*, vol. 1, New York 1991.

Sagan, Eli, *The Honey and the Hemlock: Democracy and Paranoia in Ancient Athens and Modern America*, New York 1991.

Sinclair, R.K., *Democracy and Participation in Athens*, Cambridge 1988.

Stanton, G.R., *Athenian Politics C. 800-500 B.C. A Sourcebook*, London and New York 1990.

Starr, Chester G., *Individual and Community: The Rise of the Polis, 800-500 B.C.*, New York 1986.

—, *The Birth of Athenian Democracy: The Assembly in the Fifth Century B.C.*, New York 1990.

Stone, I.F., *The Trial of Socrates*, Boston 1988.

Strauss, B.S., *Athens After the Peloponnesian War*, Ithaca 1986.

Vernant, Jean-Pierre, *The Origins of Greek Thought*, Ithaca 1982.

Whitehead, David, *The Demes of Attica, 508/7 - Ca. 250 B.C.*, Princeton 1986.

Wood, Ellen Meiksins, *Peasant-Citizen and Slave: The Foundations of Athenian Democracy*, London 1988.